CROYA
PRESS

Empowering Teens:

A Guide to Developing a Community Based Youth Organization

Elaine Doremus Slayton
CROYA

Croya Press
400 Hastings Road
Lake Forest, IL 60045
fax: 847-615-4251
www.CROYA.com

Publisher's Cataloging-in-Publication
(Provided by Quality Books, Inc.)

Slayton, Elaine Doremus.
    Empowering teens : a guide to developing a community-based youth organization / Elaine Doremus Slayton. -- 1st ed.
    p. cm.
    Includes bibliographical references.
    LCCN: 00-132080
    ISBN: 0-615-11164-5

    1. C.R.O.Y.A. (Committee Representing Our Young Adults) 2. Youth--Services for--Illinois--Lake Forest. 3. Social work with youth--Illinois--Lake Forest. I. C.R.O.Y.A. (Committee Representing Our Young Adults) II. Title.

HV1437L18S63 2000   362.7'09773'21
                    QBI00-473

Book Production by Cypress House

Frontispiece by George Steinwald
Line art page 162 by Jeanne Tanner
Cover Design by Gopa Design & Illustration
Cover image by Fitzgerald Photography, Lake Forest, Il

Disclaimer

This book was created to provide information about working effectively with teenagers (grades 7–12). It is sold with the understanding that the publisher and author are not engaged in rendering legal, counseling or other professional services. If legal or other expert assistance is required, the advice of competent professionals should be sought.

It is not the purpose of this book to reprint all the material that is otherwise available to those in need of information on the subject of teenagers or youth organizations. The information herein is derived from the author's research on the subject of one youth organization and its methods, and is intended to complement, supplement and amplify the existing body of literature pertaining to youth and youth groups. You are urged to read all the available material, learn as much as possible about the subject, and tailor the information to your specific needs. For more information, please explore the many resources available in your local library and on the Internet, as well as those additional resources mentioned in this book.

There is no quick, simple formula for working effectively with teenagers. Those who wish to become involved in this complex and sometimes frustrating subject must expect to invest considerable time and energy in order to derive the maximum benefit, both for teenagers and the adults to whom they look for guidance.

Every effort has been made to make this book as complete and as accurate as possible. However, there may be mistakes, both typographical and in content. Therefore, this text should be used only as a general guide, and not as the ultimate source of information about teenagers and youth organizations. Furthermore, this book may contain information that is current only up to the printing date.

The purpose of this book is to share ideas and methods and to inspire those seeking to work effectively with youth. The author and the Committee Representing Our Young Adults shall have neither liability nor responsibility to any person or entity with respect to any loss or damage caused, or alleged to have been caused, directly or indirectly, by the information contained in this book.

If you do not wish to be bound by the above, you may return this book to the publisher for a full refund.

Foreword

AS THE TITLE SUGGESTS, this book presents a valuable guide for those
who are, individually or as a community, anxious to develop a
community-based youth organization. The audience need not,
however, be so limited. Anyone concerned with the apparent teenage disconnect with today's society, so starkly illustrated as a new
century begins, will find it challenging of old ways and exciting
with new ones. It is a story set in an affluent suburb, yet one that
has applications for any community ready to accept the challenge
presented by teen-age anomie. And it is a case study, filled with
lessons learned by failures as well as successes, as dedicated individuals in this mid-west setting sought and continue to seek to
empower youth and to provide those developmental assets which
so compellingly affect behavior.

Here the reader will find the story of how Lake Forest, Illinois
and its neighboring community of Lake Bluff set out twenty years
ago to confront a community crisis ignited by teenage suicides
and fueled by all those other problems that this age group illustrated in the late 1970s. These two communities joined together in
1980 in establishing an organization known as CROYA, an acro-
nym for Committee Representing Our Young Adults. The author,
frequently relying on the words of students and others involved
in this effort, has drawn a compelling picture of organizational
growth, tracing its evolution over the past twenty years of its existence. It is no false claim to state that, today, CROYA is highly
visible and widely recognized in its communities and praised by
youth and adults alike for its contributions to teenage life. Such
recognition has won its status as a well established and autonomous government organization, striving to meet a variety of youth
needs with rare understanding and community support.

I was privileged to serve as the first chairperson of CROYA,
appointed to that position in 1980. My CROYA colleagues, both
adults and high school students, felt in those early years a sense

of excitement and participated enthusiastically in conversations and actions supported by research undertaken by the faculty and students of the college that I then served as president. We made mistakes, to be sure, as we walked along untrod paths, and as we stumbled it was almost invariably the teenagers themselves who picked us up. At no time, however, did enthusiasm wane, or excitement falter. We knew then, as those involved with CROYA know today, that a community's strength relies on the well being of its youth; indeed, that the promise of tomorrow's society lies with today's teenagers.

Since those early days, CROYA has evolved, as this book illustrates, under the leadership and participation of both adults and students, unfortunately too numerous to receive due individual recognition here. These times were not always easy, nor the accomplishments predictable. Student participation grew slowly at first, and not until they felt that it was truly *their* organization, was it fully accepted. It took great faith on the part of the city fathers to grant, in time, the autonomy which CROYA today claims, and the budget support which CROYA today enjoys, faith built upon program results slowly but surely achieved. Concurrently, CROYA leaders developed strong relationships with other organizations in town, often silently but in time convincingly. In no case was this more important, as the following pages indicate, than the developed relationship of mutual support void of competition with the schools, both public and private.

As these administrative struggles were going on, something very exciting was happening within the organization; the evolution of what is know within CROYA as the "CROYA process;" a process in which "everything starts with youth, is driven by youth, is for youth, and succeeds or fails because of youth." The reader of this book will come to understand that this is what truly differentiates CROYA, that this dominates CROYA, and that this is what empowers the youth of Lake Forest, Lake Bluff and Knollwood.

One will find in this book, so ably written by Ms. Slayton, a clear example of how three communities came together as one, created an organization out of a crisis, and fostered and nurtured an organization concerned with meeting teen needs. It is difficult to imagine a community that could not benefit from understanding what has evolved over these past twenty years in Lake Forest and its sister communities. This book details programs and illustrates staff functions by way of examples for others to follow, and shares in print what has already often been shared in conversation by CROYA staff with concerned communities.

The issues which brought about the establishment of CROYA in 1980 have, if anything, become more exaggerated as youth search for empowerment within their communities today, and develop through that empowerment constructive and acceptable behavior patterns. The excitement of CROYA, which one finds here in the words of its students is motivating and energizing regardless of a community's location. The reader will be well rewarded and uplifted by what this book says about the youth of today.

Eugene Hotchkiss
President Emeritus, Lake Forest College
Lake Forest, IL
January 2000

Preface

FOUNDED IN 1980, the Committee Representing Our Young Adults has evolved into a thriving, firmly established youth agency serving the teens of Lake Forest, Lake Bluff and Knollwood, Illinois. This book strives to share CROYA's formula for success, and present practical how-to details about how individual events, programs, youth and staff members come together to form an organization that is *for* youth and *run by* youth. It is an effort to educate parents, educators, young people, and communities at large about the incredible opportunities that exist for connecting with and providing positive experiences for today's youth. An account of CROYA's early days, when community leaders and volunteers were learning by trial and error, not only documents the history, it provides insight into the growth process that was so critical to CROYA's continued existence and success.

In researching this work, the author observed CROYA's activities for one full year — attending virtually every meeting, program, social event, outing, retreat and community service effort — in order to fully grasp the scope and nature of the organization's work as well as CROYA staff's relationship and process for working with teenagers. In addition, the author interviewed numerous people who have been involved with CROYA over the years — early founders and staff, board members, educators, city leaders, current staff and youth, parents and CROYA "alumni." The author attended youth conferences with CROYA staff, visited and interviewed youth agencies in other communities, and accessed current research and published material pertaining to youth (see References) in order to present an historical, accurate and living account of the agency.

It is important to stress that CROYA's model for working with youth is shared in an effort to capture the essence of its work with young people. Other communities are encouraged to use the programs and methods described herein as they see fit, developing youth organizations that fit the unique characteristics and needs of *their* youth.

Acknowledgements

TREMENDOUS THANKS ARE DUE to the people who helped make this book a reality. First and foremost, I am indebted to the young people of CROYA, who unconditionally invited me into their world, exposing themselves to an unfamiliar, non-CROYA adult who was always taking notes. They shared their thoughts and feelings about being teens and about being CROYA kids, and demonstrated without inhibition the real CROYA so that I might write about it. They raised a large portion of the funds to commission and publish this work, giving up monies they might have spent on more "fun" things. They attended special "book" meetings from the start, periodically read segments of the manuscript, gave feedback, and unabashedly shared their true selves so that I might understand and share the magic of CROYA. In short, they trusted me because the CROYA adults whom youth came to trust asked them to.

In addition to the monies raised by CROYA youth, Susan Garrett, Illinois House Representative for the 59th District, secured a substantial grant to help complete the CROYA book project. In addition, a generous gift was given by Mr. Wally Allen, Jr., of the Waldo Allen family who donated the funds in 1987 to build the CROYA facility. CROYA is extremely grateful for their help in allowing us to professionally publish and publicize this book.

I am also extremely grateful to community members who unhesitatingly gave of their time to talk to me and supply me with information. These include former CROYA pioneers and staff members Dr. Eugene Hotchkiss, Dr. Robert Metcalf, and Scott Bermingham, former and current city leaders Frank Farwell and Robert Kiely, and CROYA adult board members, school personnel, parents and volunteers, all of whom contributed to CROYA's genesis and its continued existence and success. Without their memories and documents I could not have pieced together the history of

CROYA in order to present a thorough understanding of how and why CROYA came to be and is what it is today.

Lastly, I am indebted to current CROYA director Kamy Daddono, and former director Margot Martino, who conceived the idea of a book and shared with me their visions for it. In addition, the current CROYA staff—Todd, Lynne, Gretchen, Joanne and Barbara—helped me in countless ways to learn about and research the many facets of CROYA. They gave me the time and material I requested, helped facilitate meetings with young people, read and gave feedback on drafts of the work in progress, answered thousands of questions, and made me feel part of the special bond they share and create with CROYA youth.

CONTENTS

1

CROYA Now and Then

(ॐ)

"If we as a nation are to successfully promote the healthy growth and development of all young adolescents, we must focus not on what is wrong with young adolescents, but rather on what is right."

— Peter Scales, *A Portrait of Young Adolescents in the 1990s*, Search Institute[†]

CROYA Today

"This is the first time in 25 years that anyone has asked me to talk to the kids."

IT'S JANUARY—FOR CROYA, the beginning of its nineteenth year. At 5:30 on a Wednesday evening, twenty-five youths gather for a dinner meeting at the CROYA facility. This is not unusual; the organization's Junior and Senior Executive Committees, made up of young people and staff, often meet to plan events, conduct business, and enjoy socializing with peers.

Tonight, however, the youths are being asked to do something they've never done before: Lake Forest's police chief has retired after more than twenty years' service, and the city has retained a recruiter to find applicants qualified to fill the position. They are soliciting input from the community by having the recruiter meet such groups as seniors and

---

[†] See References, page 160

business owners. One of these groups is the youth of CROYA.

As the meeting begins, the kids, eating pizza and sweets, sit in a circle on the floor, giving their attention to their guest. The recruiter begins by saying, "This is the first time in twenty-five years that anyone has asked me to talk to the kids." He's obviously already impressed by this testament to CROYA's uniqueness and success. It addresses the core of CROYA philosophy: *Start with youth.* This is an ideal opportunity to do just that, by seeking input from the community's young people about what kind of police chief *they* want and need.

A big step for CROYA, this is an important opportunity to improve upon communication and the relationship between youth and police. Young people often perceive that they are singled out for "just driving around" or "hanging out uptown."

Given this chance to offer input, CROYA youth are up to the task. Through the "CROYA Process," they've learned to be open and vocal about their feelings and opinions, and this forum is no different. Aware of the community demographics, they tell the recruiter that they want a "visible" police chief who demonstrates sensitivity to the fact that the community's affluence gives it unique characteristics and needs.

Candidly, they say they'd like a chief who demonstrates respect for young people and is seriously committed to the community's youth programs. They want someone who'll be "actively involved" and will come to some youth programs and speak informally with them to get a real understanding of "where they are at." They feel strongly, for example, that the police chief should attend the Donut Bowl or the Donut Cup—annual football and hockey games between youths and police officers. They also want a chief who demonstrates consistency regarding reasons for stopping or ticketing kids. Lastly, they request that the chief have "good people skills" and be willing to hold an annual roundtable with the community's youths.

The fact that these young people want to be part of a regular dialogue with authorities reveals their sincere desire to work things out through a healthy process. As CROYA's director Kamy Daddono stated at the end of the session, "Young people want to work with the police in ways that are creative and not adversarial."

While one not familiar with CROYA's process of working with the young might be astonished at the seriousness, forethought, straightforwardness and depth of feeling of these high school students, this is precisely what the organization has become known for among the young and throughout the larger community.

CROYA has explicit mission and vision statements:

CROYA's Mission Statement

Lake Forest and Lake Bluff strive to provide a high quality of life for their young adults in an environment that promotes their growth and development. Lake Forest and Lake Bluff charge CROYA with the task of helping the young adults identify and meet their own needs.

Accordingly, CROYA will be used by the young adults to identify their needs or problems and to communicate them to the appropriate resources. CROYA will assist the communities' resources, coordinate and organize themselves to best meet these youth-identified needs. CROYA will, itself, provide programs to meet these youth-identified needs in conjunction with other resources.

CROYA's Vision Statement

In the next five to ten years, CROYA will be affected by changing youth needs, limited funding, adult-perceived community needs, and youth participation in CROYA programs. We can meet these challenges by continuing to develop avenues in which youth can identify their own needs, establish additional programs to meet the identified needs and act as ombudsman between the community and the youth in addressing changing social issues that affect Lake Forest and Lake Bluff. In ten years, CROYA plans to expand in creating additional opportunities for youth to invest in themselves and their community, and the community to invest in their youth.

CROYA's History

"Lake Forest and Lake Bluff has always had at its core an interest in doing what's best for kids and families."

— Scott Bermingham, former CROYA Adult Board chair

Founded in 1980, CROYA has become a vital youth agency for the communities of Lake Forest, Lake Bluff and Knollwood, Illinois, which are located on the shore of Lake Michigan about thirty miles north of Chicago. Funded by tax dollars, private donations, and fundraising monies, CROYA exists on a level above most youth organizations. Boasting its own facility, four full-time staff members and one part-time secretary, CROYA is hooked into every vital entity connected to the youth of the community. This includes schools, community-wide service organizations such as the Volunteer Bureau and the United Way, and community events. CROYA sponsors and co-sponsors events, coordinates participation in community service, and gets involved wherever they think CROYA's presence and the involvement of youth would fulfill its mission. CROYA's success and the respect it has earned from this and neighboring communities has been achieved through the vision and dedication of many people over the years. As CROYA's director, Kamy Daddono, puts it, "CROYA has the pulse of the kids of this community."

The Impetus for CROYA

CROYA began in the mid-1970s in a community hit hard by problems with its youth: several teen suicides, drug and alcohol abuse, a teen gang called "The Losers," and vandalism. The movie *Ordinary People* (Paramount Pictures, 1980), which was set and filmed in Lake Forest and neighboring communities, told the story of one affluent teenager's attempted suicide. This may have been the decisive factor that compelled residents of Lake Forest and Lake Bluff to look beneath the surface and take a hard look at what was going on with their children.

In 1976 the City of Lake Forest commissioned a study by the Lake County Youth Service Bureau, for the purpose of assessing youth needs and the community's resources and to make recommendations to the community. Their report specifically recommended the formation of a "youth council" directly responsible to the city council. Further, the study recommended that this group should be community-based and have youth as its only focus. Also emphasized in the recommendations were "more alternative activities" and at least one fulltime position—"a non-threatening, low-key, informal counselor"—to be hired by the city.

Other concerned organizations became involved as well. In 1979, the League of Women Voters of Lake Forest completed a review of Lake Forest youth services. This study recommended that the city act upon the 1976 report as soon as possible. In addition, the Association of Parents and Teachers (APT) held a well attended community meeting in 1979 for the sole purpose of discussing the youth of Lake Forest.

Thus, in 1979, Frank J. Waldeck, then mayor of Lake Forest, formed an *ad hoc* committee consisting of Aldermen Frank Farwell and John Hennessy, and City Manager John F. Fischbach. Specifically, their task was to "consider the proper role of the City in responding to the needs of its young people." Their consideration and investigation included more than twenty meetings, including a public hearing, and input from residents, professionals, and interested parties.

Nine months after its inception, the *ad hoc* committee presented "The Report of the Ad Hoc Committee on Youth Matters to the Lake Forest City Council," which concluded, "The City of Lake Forest indeed has a role in the developmental process of its young people and in the nurturing of the family unit within Lake Forest." In order to address this role, the committee recommended, among other things, "the establishment of a Committee Representing Our Young Adults (CROYA)," emphasizing, "CROYA should be a citizens' committee, operating independently and unfettered by bureaucratic interference and reporting only to the Ad Hoc committee at quarterly intervals."

The CROYA committee was thus established and formed of citizens appointed by the mayor of Lake Forest and the village president of Lake Bluff. That original governing body included: one student and one parent from each high school; one parent from the junior high school district; the director of Lake Forest Recreation department; one member-at-large from both Lake Forest and Lake Bluff; and the chair, who was the president of Lake Forest College. They divided into subcommittees with the task of researching youth problems and needs and dialoging ideas for addressing those needs. These subcommittees focused on areas such as "youth programs," "communications," "resource publications" and "research." This original committee of nine was very different, both in its mission and level of hands-on involvement, from the current adult board of CROYA. (See Chapter Four for explanation of Adult Board.)

What's in a name?

C.R.O.Y.A. stands for the Committee Representing Our Young Adults. A result of careful consideration by Frank Farwell, mayor of Lake Forest during CROYA's genesis in the late 1970s and early '80s, the name carries significant meaning. As Mr. Farwell explains, he and other early visionaries wanted "to impart a feeling of warmth" and create a name that "dignified youth." They wanted to refer to young people not as "kids" but as "young adults." Additionally, they wanted the name to denote CROYA's purpose, i.e., to "represent young adults." The focus was to be the community's youth, and it was paramount that the name communicate this clearly. Lastly, Farwell explains, they wanted a name with a "lyrical quality" and five letters rather than four. CROYA is pronounced "croi´-yuh."

While the founders of CROYA were not necessarily cognizant of some of the word's possible root meanings, at a dinner hosted to solicit information for this book, Barat College president Lucy Moros pointed out:

"croire" [krwar], the Latin root, means *to believe; to think,* and *"croyance"* [krwayans], the French word means *belief; creed; faith*

These qualities have since become synonymous with CROYA—for the youth, the staff, city officials, and the community at large.

The Early Years

The newly formed CROYA focused primarily on the young people referred to as "losers" and "burn-outs," and on youth with special needs. They continued to meet with influential community organizations, such as the American Association of University Women (AAUW), The League of Women Voters, the Junior League, Newcomers, Rotary, and the American Legion, with the goal of obtaining as much information and insight as possible to address this problem head-on.

Dr. Eugene Hotchkiss, then president of Lake Forest College and one of CROYA's pioneers, recalls "CROYA's task in the beginning was to design and implement programs of interest for young people." What they found, however, was that young people did not necessarily want or respond to programs created *for* them. Dr. Hotchkiss wrote in his 1986 "Evaluation and Assessment" report, "Too often activities were imposed on the youth, in which many participated but felt little sense of ownership." A mandatory assembly on drugs, for example, held at Lake Forest High School and co-sponsored by Pace (Junior League) and CROYA, featured a noted expert on drugs. While the intention may have been to educate youth and open a dialogue between teens and adults, students were angry and offended at being forced to listen to a lecture when they felt they already knew the facts about drugs.

These early lessons were reinforced by the observation in the soon-to-be-published *Youth Needs Assessment* that, "The prolonged condition of semi-childhood becomes burdensome for people physically and intellectually mature, yet restricted in their access to decision-making power over issues which directly affect them."

Youth Needs Assessment

This, in connection with CROYA's quest for information with which to act, led CROYA to commission Lake Forest College to conduct a *Youth Needs Assessment* in 1981. This study was developed and conducted by a research team of two sociology professors at Lake Forest College, Dr. Gene Muehlbauer and Dr. Arlene Eskilson, with Laura Dodder, a student researcher. It was to recommend, among other things, "more activities for youth" as well as some help for the "significant proportion of our young people (who) are overwhelmed by multiple pressures..." This was a significant finding. While the impetus for CROYA may have been an increased awareness of youth involved with drugs, alcohol, and violence, most young people simply needed help dealing with the daily stresses of life as a teenager in an affluent community. In their section, "Some Comments on the Condition of Youth in America," the authors observe:

> *Some of the difficulties faced by youth are particular to the communities in which they live. Young people growing up in affluent suburbs are subject to pressures that reflect their distinctive environment. To a great extent, they share these pressures with their parents, albeit at a different level. The strong emphasis on achievement which parents may feel in their world is reflected in the child's world, especially in the school. Many children of highly successful parents also believe that they must live up to that same level of accomplishment. While the emphasis on competition and winning prepares many students for the adult world, it has negative effects for some of the participants. Not all personalities have equal capacities for competitive stress, nor do all achieve best under such circumstances. In adolescence, especially, children are vulnerable to severe erosion of their self-esteem. If a child's social environment is unresponsive to the need for understanding in the face of failure, however defined, there can be extremely debilitating short- and sometimes long-term consequences for his or her self-esteem.*

In their introduction to the report, the authors also observe, "It is a period of life fraught with built-in contradictions. People in this category are neither adults nor children, thus leading to a confusion of expectations from self and from others." CROYA youth today talk about the same issues that surfaced nearly two decades ago in the *Youth Needs Assessment*: volume of homework; expectations of parents and teachers; pressure to get good grades and be successful; as well as peer pressure to drink, use drugs or become sexually active.

In the study, students communicated their feeling that "They have little ability to influence decisions about their recreational needs, and both students and parents indicate that youth should have more input than they do now." Respondents to the study also expressed a desire for, among other things, a "youth center." CROYA has become a place to get away from these pressures temporarily, to talk to adults who understand, to be with other kids who feel the same things, and to be accepted no matter what.

Changes in Philosophy, Direction and Program

According to Dr. Hotchkiss, "During those first six years CROYA underwent numerous changes in philosophy, direction, program, etc." In early 1981, CROYA had hired a full-time youth worker, who was a trained counselor, devoted to outreach and counseling, and responsible for directing program activities as well as responding to the psychological needs of those youth needing help. The *Youth Needs Assessment* was to confirm that "Parent support is highest for alcohol and drug counseling, each of which is rated of high importance by three-fourths or more of the parents replying to the survey." But typically, youth are reluctant to approach someone labeled as a "counselor." As a "youth worker" with counseling training and experience, it was hoped that this person could establish relationships with youth through youth programming, but would also be prepared to step into the counseling role when needed. While this first youth worker was able to influence some youths, the number was very small. It was later determined that this program was not meeting the needs of the great number of young people.

This was troubling because, as the *Youth Needs Assessment* had uncovered, "A far smaller percent of young people indicate that they would turn to their parents for help with such issues as drinking or drug problems, family problems, or problems connected with sexual activity." This was compared with their propensity to seek parental advice in areas such as grades, emotional or medical problems or problems getting along with friends." One question that arose from this was "To whom could youth turn, then, when faced with the serious issues of drugs, alcohol, etc?" This was the gap that CROYA was attempting to fill, but having some difficulty in finding the way. (See Chapter Two.)

Then, CROYA decided to turn its attention to serving increasing numbers of youth and to providing additional alternative youth activities as a way to reach out to young people and to develop an attitude of trust. In 1983, they replaced the counselor with an "activities person" responsible for working with young adults. And, while more emphasis was placed on programming for youth during this time, at least one critical element was missing: the presence of an adult or adults who could really relate to young adults by gaining their trust and confidence and being there to listen when they had problems. While the activities staff person had good intentions, he also demonstrated difficulty in connecting to youth in an appropriate way. As one parent remembers, "One of the first directors came in wearing a suit and carrying a briefcase. He couldn't connect with youth." This marked a turning point for CROYA.

Today, current CROYA director Kamy Daddono talks about the importance of sending a clear message in the way she and the staff dress. When she has a meeting in the community, for which she dresses professionally, she also brings a change of clothes to CROYA for the remainder of the day. Wearing casual clothes, whether jeans and tee shirts or the latest fashion craze of cargo pants and hooded sweatshirts, is a step toward removing barriers between youth and adults. While this may seem superficial, it is one essential element in getting on the same level as youth, the place where trust and dialogue begin. Pioneering former director Margot Martino also recalls "dressing the part" during the mid-1980s when CROYA was still struggling to prove itself. She would wear what she called her "uniform" of sweatpants and sweatshirts to the CROYA office (located in City Hall at that time) and also to staff meetings with other city officials. The message was intended for adults as well as teens—starting with youth means getting on their level and fitting into their world. Dress is an important ingredient of this philosophy.

The Teenage Placement Service (TAPS—see Chapter Seven) was also conceived and put into operation around this time. It was a positive step in answering a clearly stated need and involving youth, but CROYA was still not entirely successful in bringing the youth of the community into the life of CROYA. According to Dr. Hotchkiss' 1986 report, "Perhaps the greatest accomplishment in those early years can be said to be the increased awareness of youth needs within the adult communities of Lake Forest and Lake Bluff, which CROYA's existence and its work engendered in schools and churches, in community and civic organizations, and even within families."

Turning Points

It seems unanimous among people involved with CROYA in the 1980s that the real turning point for CROYA came when Margot Martino became involved, first as a volunteer, then as head of the board, and finally as director in 1984. As Frank Farwell, former mayor of Lake Forest puts it, "Margot Martino just wandered in one day off the street, saying that she liked to work with kids and wanted to be involved somehow." At first, as a volunteer, she often held meetings with as few as six youths in attendance. They met in various places, among them the Gorton Community Center and sometimes her own home. She remembers "bowling in the hallways of my house," when there was nowhere else to meet. She baked cookies for the kids and acted as their strongest advocate within the community.

Dr. Hotchkiss emphasizes that it was because of Mrs. Martino that "CROYA became an organization which listened to the youth while hearing adults as well." It was she who, when adults wanted to step in and take control, insisted that CROYA should be youth-centered and run by youth. At one point, CROYA was nearly absorbed into the Recreation Department of Lake Forest. It seemed to make sense to a lot of people that it be housed under recreation, not as a separate entity within the city structure reporting to the city manager. Some adults saw it simply as "programming activities" for youth, which seemed to correspond more naturally with recreation. But several CROYA advocates, including Margot Martino (CROYA's director), Scott Bermingham (CROYA's adult board chair) and the CROYA youth were successful at convincing the city manager to allow them to remain autonomous. Under Mrs. Martino's vision and leadership, CROYA built a base of student support, strengthened TAPS, supported the Mam'selle program, and facilitated student-led efforts to bring many alternative activities, such as concerts on the beach, dances, and car washes, to the community's young people.

As CROYA attendance grew, they needed to find a suitable permanent meeting place. The *Youth Needs Assessment* had observed, "Young people desire to congregate in places away from adult view." Early staff members had office space in City Hall, but that location did not lend itself to youth meetings or youth "dropping by," and occasionally their presence in City Hall elicited complaints. With no place to call their own, CROYA borrowed space for meetings in such places as the Gorton Community Center and the Masonic Temple. While this was sometimes inconvenient, with last-minute room changes and locked doors to contend with, it did help expand the community's awareness of CROYA, developing goodwill and trust of youth. But not having its own place was preventing CROYA from realizing its full potential as a youth agency.

Fortuitously, in January 1987, CROYA received a gift of $200,000 from the Waldo Morgan Allen Charities, Inc. Its purpose was to construct a headquarters and activity area for CROYA on the Deer Path Park property. WMAC was a trust established by Mr. Waldo Morgan Allen, and administered after his death by his wife, Mrs. Mary Allen, and their two children. Mr. Allen had specifically wanted the trust to benefit the young people of Lake Forest. After extensive consultation and considerations, Mrs. Allen and her children decided that funding a CROYA facility was the best way to provide long-term benefits to the young people of Lake Forest and Lake Bluff.

The CROYA facility, which adjoins the Lake Forest Recreation Center, was once a dance studio that was renovated and enlarged in 1987. Designed with considerable youth input, it has become a friendly home away from home for many young people. It boasts a large family room, a full kitchen, and a Resource Gallery. They have a television, VCR, and stereo system with youth-selected music. A reception area and four offices line one side of the facility, with staff office doors always open in welcome. While connected to the recreation center with access through one door, it is very separate as an entity. Much of CROYA's autonomy and success have been attributed to having its own facility. Given the opportunity to "stand on their own," both literally and figuratively, CROYA has had to prove its commitment, dedication, and ability to help "youth meet youth's needs." CROYA's facility has symbolized its independence and responsibility to youth and the community at large.

Current CROYA

It is important to note that CROYA is not a club, nor is it set up like a drop-in center. No application, signup, membership or fee is required to attend CROYA meetings and events (except specific fees for some special programs like retreats, outings or dances). CROYA is open to all youth in grades seven through twelve residing in Lake Forest, Lake Bluff or Knollwood. It is the CROYA Process (See Chapter Three) for working with youth that draws them into the CROYA community. Holding regular weekly youth meetings, CROYA provides ample opportunity for youth to become involved through programs, events, and service projects. Any student is welcome to stop by whenever CROYA's doors are open: weekdays from about 8:30 A.M. to 5:00 P.M., two to three weekday evenings when youth meetings or other programs take place, and many weekends when special events are planned. Inside, they'll find a casual working environment with staff busy meeting and planning upcoming meetings and events. It is a safe place for youth and a place to connect with caring adults.

Since the mid-eighties, CROYA has continued to grow and evolve into the thriving, vital agency it is today. It holds weekly youth meetings with both junior high and senior high youth, hosts regular and annual social events just for kids, co-sponsors many programs with schools and other not-for-profit community groups, conducts regular community service projects, offers semi-annual retreats to Wisconsin, and much more. Everywhere that youth are, CROYA is. The agency's place among youth and within the community is firmly established.

2

Inevitable Lessons Learned

ⱭⱭⱭ

"Every failure precipitated growth, leading CROYA in new directions. The failures were not really failures, because we learned so much from them. Without those opportunities, CROYA couldn't be where it is today."

— Margot Martino, CROYA's first director

Early Direction and the First CROYA Staff

IN ANY PILOT PROGRAM there is pressure to demonstrate results quickly, which creates a dilemma for communities attempting to build a foundation of trust and relationships with youth. It simply is not a quick-fix situation. It takes perseverance and time. While CROYA was not established as a pilot program per se, resources had been committed to it and community leaders were eager to demonstrate that strides were being made. They had allocated funding and had engaged the time and effort of many community leaders. In addition, they were still sensitive to the recent events that had precipitated CROYA's birth.

The executive committee of CROYA hired its first youth worker in January 1981. The arrangement was unusual in that he was not a direct employee of the City of Lake Forest. Working with an agency called Family Services of South Lake County, CROYA contracted the services of a counselor to work approximately thirty hours per week for a one-year contract in fulfilling their mission. While the youth worker was paid by Lake Forest and given direction from the CROYA board, he reported directly to his agency. Most of his work was onsite at schools and at the recreation department, where he was provided a desk and a phone, and he met with the CROYA board periodically for direction. But this arrangement later proved to be problematic for various reasons.

In retrospect, the problems stemmed from differing opinions as to the youth counselor's role and responsibilities. The counselor saw his objectives as twofold: First, he wanted to concentrate on outreach and what he called "informal counseling." This translated into hanging around where kids did—lunchrooms, the "pit" at the high school, and the recreation center game room. His objective was to build relationships with youth as a means of establishing trust and working towards more involvement with youth. To his credit, this is an ingredient of CROYA's successful model for working with youth today.

His second objective was to form what were called "youth program committees" with the goal of helping youth to make decisions about what *they* wanted to do with their time and then make them a reality. While this was a slow process, he was successful at working with kids to plan and execute several dances, and later a rock concert. The important outcome in this element of the strategy was not the activities that were planned, but *the process by which youth are empowered to work together and plan their own activities*. The theory is that through this process, the alienation that often leads to substance abuse, gang involvement, and depression can be reduced. This still holds true today and has evolved into what is known as The CROYA Process. (See Chapter Three.)

Tensions developed when the city and the CROYA executive committee began to pressure the youth worker to "be more visible" in his efforts, and to "plan more activities for youth." Much of the work being done was "behind the scenes," so to speak. While hanging out with kids playing Frisbee, pool or video games was critical to the relationship and trust-building, it was not necessarily an obvious or quick "fix" for the problems as perceived by the community.

About six months after joining CROYA, the youth worker was given his first job description, which revealed the differences between his priorities and CROYA's. While his emphasis was on outreach and youth program committees, CROYA highlighted "community relations" and "special events" as its first two objectives. Outreach and what they termed "special problem" groups (such as discussion groups) were lower on their list of priorities. While the youth worker's contract was renewed after one year for another six-month term, he eventually left. CROYA moved on in its development as an agency.

It is interesting to note that, twenty years later *CROYA's core philosophy for working with youth is building relationships.* What makes the agency successful is that young people run it. Youth subcommittees are central to every event planned. (See Chapter Three.) The strategies of that first youth worker would later come to be a part of CROYA's basic strategy for working with youth.

The communities of Lake Forest, Lake Bluff, and Knollwood are supportive of that process today. They do not micro-manage how the staff does its job, nor do they usurp the authority of CROYA's adult board. Staff members have specific responsibilities and quantifiable objectives, using a tracking system to document their activities. CROYA has also clarified its role with respect to counseling, choosing not to have a staff person acting in that capacity. (See Chapter Twelve.)

This trust and empowerment of CROYA and the youth have come with time, patience, and proven results. It is understandable that a community reacting to serious problems with its youth would be eager to address the problems quickly and visibly. It is also fair to say that not everyone, no matter how good their intentions, is qualified to know how best to connect with youth. CROYA staff has demonstrated a level of expertise—based on their training, education, and natural abilities to connect with youth—that not every community leader or even every parent possesses. It is incumbent upon the community to respect youth workers as professionals in their field and give them the time, resources and support to demonstrate results.

Evolution of the Adult Board

The original board, which is different from the original committee, was very high-powered. City officials and community advocates who had put their faith in the inception of CROYA wanted to lend the most influential community resources to the effort. This worked well for a while. As a fledgling agency that had its share of community skeptics, CROYA needed the support of respected community leaders who would help access the community resources that would allow it to develop and grow. That first board grew very large, at one point having as many as thirty members. Among other things, they mapped out philosophically what they envisioned a youth agency to be.

This board evolved into an adult board that was more of a "working board." They became involved with youth one-on-one, working directly with the youth committee. They chaperoned events, attended retreats, and provided psychological support. It soon became apparent, however, that the young people had become their own working board. Utilizing the CROYA Process (See Chapter Three), kids had learned to set their own direction, formed subcommittees to make things happen, and took the credit and accountability for results.

Because of this, the board's role eventually shifted from a working board to the resource board that it remains today. The adult board essentially provides input and helps CROYA obtain the resources it needs, including funding, facilities for events like Summer Jam, and influential authority figures on matters close to the youth of CROYA. The board was willing to step back, becoming less visible in the actual workings of CROYA, because youth had proven that they would do things in an appropriate manner. The CROYA youth had begun to earn the trust of the adult board and the community.

Events that Backfired

"Hope for the best. Prepare for the worst."

While CROYA staff and youth are very fortunate that they have learned mostly from successes over the years, there have been some events that simply flopped for one reason or another. CROYA staff member Lynne Siegel explains, "Sometimes you think you're going to have forty kids for an event, but only a few show up. So you send the bus home and make the best of the situation. But you never really know."

CROYA's first Summer Jam

"The community was terrified of a "rock concert." I think some envisioned another Woodstock."

— Margot Martino, CROYA's first director

In 1981, when CROYA had one youth worker on staff and a couple of volunteers helping out, the youth of CROYA really wanted to have a rock concert. Music, it turned out, was the one common thread among all kids no matter to what group they did or did not belong. Adults working with the youth were faced with a dilemma: They had been sending the message that CROYA listens to youth, that CROYA was youth's vehicle to do things that they wanted. The adults also knew that "selling" a rock concert to CROYA's adult board and city officials wouldn't be easy. But this was an opportunity to prove something, both to the young people and to the community at large, so early leaders of CROYA decided to move forward with the idea and "test the waters."

Understandably, city officials and CROYA's adult board were at first reluctant to approve a concert, sensing possibilities for disaster, but CROYA's adult spokespeople convinced the adult board to listen to a proposal that the youth would prepare. They assured the adult board that CROYA's youth would anticipate possible problems and address those issues in the proposal. They wanted the adult board to have open minds, and see whether the young people could anticipate everything involved in putting on a rock concert and come up with a safe, viable plan. The adult board agreed to proceed "in theory" with the idea of a rock concert, promising to consider a thorough proposal by CROYA youth. Since this type of event would be "high-profile" for CROYA, the benefits of a successful event were appealing. In retrospect, former director Margot Martino remembers, "This is where the CROYA Process (See Chapter Three) was born and would become the prototype for CROYA's work in the future."

Youth volunteered to be on the concert committee. They began by making a wish list for their rock concert and what they thought needed to be done to make it happen. They met with the city manager of Lake Forest to brainstorm possible problems with their plan. The kids went back to the drawing board, taking this input back to the CROYA youth committee and discussing issues like noise, security and chaperoning. Further dividing into subcommittees, one CROYA adult board member was assigned to work with each youth subcommittee.

Committees considered various sites for the concert, including Lake Forest College, the Lake Forest High School West Campus, and Deerpath Elementary School field, noting the advantages and disadvantages of each. They sent postcards to parents, asking for chaperone volunteers, and planned a training session. They looked into busing, snow fencing, refreshments, and the possibility of holding the concert at night. The CROYA director worked with them every step of the way, playing devil's advocate when necessary to help them see when things like holding it at night were unrealistic for a first-time event of this magnitude.

At the end of this process, CROYA youth presented a proposal to the adult board and the city manager. While it might not have been typed and polished, it came from the kids and reflected their hard work and thoughtfulness in planning a responsible rock concert. The adult board was so impressed and proud that they took a risk and approved the event. But CROYA youth weren't over all the hurdles yet. Finding a location proved difficult, because both public schools turned them down. The city agreed to give them use of the field outside the recreation center.

With everything set to go, the weather looked ominous on the morning of Summer Jam. Perhaps too eager for an excuse to cancel the concert, city officials called it off despite the fact that the skies had cleared by mid-day. Youth were understandably disappointed, but felt some satisfaction in having gotten as far as they had. As it turns out, neighbors reportedly called the police that day to complain about the noise of a concert that wasn't taking place—clear evidence of the resistance some community members harbored.

Fortunately, CROYA succeeded in hosting its first Summer Jam the following summer, at the indoor field house at Lake Forest College. This time, inclement weather didn't stop them. The concert was moved from outdoors to the indoor field house, thanks to the faith and support of Eugene Hotchkiss, then president of Lake Forest College. And it was a success with no unfortunate incidents to mar the day.

The failed first Summer Jam was an important step in demonstrating youth's ability to plan a responsible rock concert. This encouraged city officials and CROYA adult board members to help make it a reality the next summer. The birth of The CROYA Process marked a transition from "risky agency" to a new level of trust and confidence in CROYA as a respected youth community.

Chemical People

Around 1983, a national movement called "Chemical People" was encouraging communities to take prevention steps against alcohol and drug abuse. They developed a brochure that individual groups could endorse as a way of circulating this information. CROYA was approached and asked if it wanted to sponsor the movement. The youth worker on staff at the time presented the idea to the youth and the adult board of CROYA. It is important to point out that the *Youth Needs Assessment* (See Chapter One) had specifically recommended that CROYA *not* align itself with any other large organized agency, group, or cause. The CROYA youth and the adult board unanimously voted "no" to becoming connected with this movement. But the CROYA youth worker decided to go ahead anyway.

The outcome threatened to destroy everything that CROYA had built in its first few years. Young people were furious. The trust that CROYA had so carefully cultivated had been broken, giving CROYA a "bad rap." This seriously threatened the survival of the youth committee and CROYA. Since then, CROYA has been careful not to make a similar mistake. Staff would never disregard the opinions or unanimous votes of the youth committees or the adult board. CROYA is careful to remain autonomous, despite the fact that it co-sponsor many events with local community organizations.

Donut Bowl and Donut Cup

In recent years, in an effort to encourage a more open relationship between police and youth, CROYA co-sponsors an annual or biannual Donut

Bowl or Donut Cup with local police departments. It takes the form of an outdoor football game or an indoor hockey game, depending on the season.

One year, CROYA and the police were having difficulty scheduling the event due to conflicts with other major events in the schools, such as sporting events and band concerts. As a result, the Donut Cup was rescheduled four times, which probably had something to do with the low turnout of CROYA youth. There was some confusion about the date, and it ended up taking place just before final exams—less-than-ideal timing. The result was that only a few youth initially showed up. The police were there with their families, and food and a hockey rink were waiting. CROYA staff and youth made some last-minute phone calls and managed to get a few more kids to come, but it was awkward and embarrassing for staff and youth present.

At a youth meeting shortly after this particular Donut Cup, youth and staff discussed, or "processed," what had happened and talked about how to avoid a reoccurrence. The consensus was that bad scheduling and a breakdown in The CROYA Process contributed to the low turnout. Scheduling is a significant factor in the success of any event, and staff spends a good deal of time checking for conflicts within the community that will hurt attendance. Of course, they can't schedule around everything, but they've learned which conflicts tend to impact their programs most, such as sports, concerts, and school plays, and they work around them as much as possible.

℅ Youth Comment on Events that Backfired

"We've had to try more than once to make things work."

"I've found that I often learn so much more from my mistakes. The cool thing about CROYA is that they don't make us feel bad; they encourage us to learn from our mistakes and to think of ways to solve our problems."

"What's that old saying? 'If at first you don't succeed, try, try and try again.'"

"Last year I was chairman of a service project. As one of my jobs, I was to call all the kids on the sign up sheet to remind them where to meet and at what time. I completely forgot and on the day of the event I confided with the staff what had happened. Instead of yelling at me, they reassured me that "things happen." We all got on the phone and called everyone on the list. As it turned out enough kids showed to make the event a success."

"Where else can we try something and not have to worry about failing?"

3

The CROYA Process

"CROYA promotes the ability of kids to take responsibility for their own actions. Kids have the ability to set their own direction."

— Scott Bermingham,
former CROYA Adult Board chair

"The CROYA Process doesn't come naturally. Turning over ownership to kids is the hardest thing to do."

— Margot Martino, CROYA's first director

PEOPLE INVOLVED WITH CROYA often refer to the "CROYA Process" when talking about the way they do things. Alumni like to use the term when comparing CROYA with clubs at college. Everyone close to CROYA intuitively knows what it means, but attempting to convey the essence of the CROYA Process so that other communities can duplicate it is not so simple. Yet it is critical, because the process is what is important, not the end results.

Too often, when community leaders and concerned parents seek to "do something to reach the youth," the immediate reaction is to create more activities for youth. Give them something to do—build a "teen center," plan some dances, or put video games in a room somewhere. In their zeal and haste to do something, well-intentioned adults fail to recognize the most critical element—that any successful programming for youth must be youth-centered for it to work. This is what CROYA has learned and perfected over the years.

Early leaders and visionaries connected with CROYA saw this, and had to fight to make others within the community see and support it. There were times when the CROYA Process was almost usurped by those who did not understand that it was not about adults programming for youth but about involving youth in the process from the ground up.

At one point in the mid-1980s, for example, it seemed like a good idea to some to put CROYA under the auspices of the recreation department. After all, they seemed to have similar objectives when viewed from the outside—they developed healthy fun activities for kids. While the recreation department serves a vital and successful role of its own, it does not do what CROYA does, but CROYA was seriously threatened at that time. Thanks to early CROYA visionaries who went to city leaders and city council meetings, pleaded on CROYA's behalf, and brought youth to meetings to speak for themselves and "the process," city leaders were finally convinced to let CROYA succeed or fail on its own.

The CROYA Process, when examined in isolation, starts with the seed of an idea. When, last spring, for example, girls who were part of a CROYA offshoot group called Girls Night Out (GNO—see Chapter Seven), suggested that summer activities just for girls would be fun, the CROYA Process was underway. Staff members keyed into the idea and discussed it among themselves. What about the idea of a girl's summer camp? What kinds of healthy, fun, educational and esteem-building activities would lend themselves to this sort of program? CROYA activities slow down in the summer and here were some young people asking for something to do. CROYA staff was listening.

At a follow-up meeting with GNO, staff approached the girls again, this time with some ideas to pitch to generate interest and to offer a springboard for more ideas from the girls. The girls were enthusiastic and began embellishing upon staff suggestions and throwing in ideas of their own. Meetings such as this might remind an outsider of what creative talents do in, for example, an advertising agency. They need ideas for a campaign; someone throws out a lead idea, no matter how far out and undeveloped; someone likes it and adds a twist; another person has different ideas and says "What about this?" The meeting progresses like this until they end up with something tangible, a conglomeration of ideas in which they all feel they share. For the GNO girls, it was a list of about ten things they were really excited about: a trip to downtown Chicago, a career day, nutrition day, day of beauty, and a sports day including a bike ride and climbing-wall, to name a few. They put their names on a list, and what they'd be willing to work on, and that was enough for that day's meeting.

Next steps included contacting the girls—in small groups after school or during their lunch breaks and by telephone—to fine-tune ideas and delegate some responsibilities. Girls in small committees made final decisions about exactly what to do downtown, what to have for lunch, and the kinds of career women with whom they would be interested in talking. They volunteered to call people, make flyers, or help out on the day of the event. The staff set a schedule, put an announcement into the last school newsletter of the year, and sent out a flyer to every incoming seventh-, eighth- and ninth-grade girl on CROYA's mailing list. The summer program was becoming a reality.

The girls felt invested in their summer program because it was theirs. Someone listened to them when they expressed ideas and helped them make it happen. The programs reflected the wants of the girls, yet focused on healthy lifestyles that also serve to build self-esteem and awareness. The girls were connected and involved throughout the summer, keeping in touch with CROYA staff and friends they might not have seen outside of school. And, they were having fun while learning responsibility and leadership.

The CROYA Process is as simple as this. *The essential ingredient—it must be youth-centered and youth driven; it must involve youth in every step of the process, especially the decision-making process.* Adults must get out of the way in order for it to work. Often this means letting youth make mistakes on their own, so that they can learn and grow through the process. When youth feel ownership, they have a stake in ensuring participation from friends and making sure that other youth "stay in line." Often it is the youth who "self-police" events, letting anyone threatening to spoil the fun or lose privileges for everyone know when their behavior is inappropriate. And staff is trained and always present if assistance and intervention are necessary.

The CROYA Process Steps:

"Recommendations throughout the process are initiated by the kids."

— Margot Martino, CROYA's first director

• **Youth suggest an idea for a program or event, or the community approaches CROYA to request help with a service project.**

- Staff listens and provides a larger forum of youth (e.g., weekly youth meeting or a special meeting) in which to further discuss the "idea." The purpose is to ascertain whether enough young people are interested and if the proposal is viable.

- The youth committee votes to proceed with the "idea."

- A subcommittee is formed of youth volunteers. Chairs and co-chairs of the committee are picked out of a hat from those who have expressed interest. This gives all youth across all grades the opportunity to lead something, without it becoming a popularity contest or becoming seniority-reliant.

- The subcommittee lists everything that the program or event entails (location, permits or permission, refreshments, guest speakers, logistics, security, chaperone needs, overhead costs, what to charge, pre-sales and promotion, transportation, schedule, materials, obstacles, etc.). The kids and staff break things down into doable parts.

- The program is further broken down into tasks. Individuals take responsibility for various aspects of the planning (refreshments, tickets and sales, promotion, set-up, contacting pertinent people or agencies, etc.).

- Staff members are present at all meetings, facilitating the process, playing devil's advocate, and sustaining the momentum.

- Future meeting dates and an overall timetable are set. Some are after school, others in the evening (also known as Dinner Meetings—see chapter on the Youth Executive Committees), sometimes during lunches at school when this helps facilitate the process. Youth are assigned deliverables for each meeting, later coming together to report on progress, discuss obstacles, ask for help, etc.

- As the program approaches, staff works closely with committee chairs to ensure youth are on schedule. In addition to meetings, frequent phone calls between staff and young people and among the kids are necessary to check on progress and attend to last-minute details. A pre-event meeting takes place close to the appointed date.

- On the day of the program or event, committee youth arrive early for setup and stay late to clean up. The youth really run the program or event, with help from staff.

- In the week(s) following an event (especially a new one), youth "process" the outcome at weekly youth meetings and sometimes via written evaluation forms. What worked and what could be improved upon are documented for the next time. Since many events are annual, CROYA youth and staff learn from each one, striving to improve upon each year's success.

☞ Youth Comment on The CROYA Process

"CROYA is a perfect parent relationship, the perfect amount of adult guidance. The staff do everything you want and nothing you don't want."

"The CROYA Process works, but without the adults, we wouldn't be here."

"The CROYA adults are our guides and connections. They do the behind the scenes work."

"Without Todd (senior high youth worker), I don't think we'd ever plan a single meeting."

"The CROYA Process is some motivated high school students with some adult help."

"Kids take pride in CROYA. They police themselves. They don't want bad things to happen."

— Margot Martino, CROYA's first director

Common Characteristics of Youth

Kids naturally look for extremes, often proposing outlandish, impractical, or crazy ideas. Typical teens challenge boundaries, limits, and adult authority. They can be self-centered, not always kind, and looking to elicit reactions. Living in the moment, teenagers tend to be visionaries, not necessarily thinking things through to foresee the ways in which their actions, words, or proposals might be unrealistic or affect others adversely.

For example, for the first Summer Jam in the early 1980s, kids wanted to light the field behind the school so they could hold the concert at night. CROYA's director listened and said, "Okay, what kinds of lights do you think you would need to light up a whole field? What planning and setup would this involve? What potential problems might this invite, and how are we going to deal with them on a budget of (X) dollars?"

CROYA staff never criticizes an idea. Instead they seek to educate youth through the process. In this case, youth saw that requesting a nighttime concert would create another obstacle to overcome with city officials, the adult board, and community members. In addition, they realized that lighting an entire field at night would be labor intensive and costly, and would require additional security procedures. After processing their proposal with staff, they decided to hold their first Summer Jam in the daytime.

Given their limited life experiences, young people are not always able to draw upon experience to make sound decisions. Using humor and playing the devil's advocate helps kids see for themselves when something is not feasible. *Humor* is especially important in working with youth. Talking it through allows kids to make surprisingly responsible decisions despite their impulse to "go for it." The kids usually see when something is not doable; the reward is when staff can model and help youth process like adults. But when they can't, staff sometimes lets them try something and learn from the experiment. This can be a learning experience for youth when a proposal doesn't work out as planned, or on the flip side, a learning experience for adults when it does.

Letting them try something extreme sometimes turns out to be a success that surprises even adults. A good example is Jell-O wrestling. CROYA youth approached the staff about having a Jell-O wrestling contest at CROYA. At first, staff felt it was a risky proposition, from how to manage all that Jell-O to how to keep it good clean fun and overcome the inferences people might make. But the young people really wanted it, so the staff agreed. They worked with youth to plan the event via the CROYA Process, anticipating the aforementioned problems. It turned out to be a huge success and extremely popular with youth. Today, Jell-O wrestling is a much-anticipated, well-attended annual event at CROYA. (See Chapter Nine.)

4

The Youth Executive Committees and the Adult Board - At the Center

∞

"CROYA works because it is run by youth. We can never lose sight of that."

— Eugene Hotchkiss, President Emeritus,
Lake Forest College

Senior High Executive Committee

IT IS EARLY SEPTEMBER and students are back at school in Lake Forest and Lake Bluff. Predictably, the bees and flies are a nuisance at the beach where the first meeting of the executive committee is being held. It's a 5:30 start time, but as early birds arrive, Todd, the senior high youth worker, and Josh, a Lake Forest High School student, are playing catch just outside the pavilion where the meeting will take place. At one point the ball skitters down the drive, threatening to go into the lake. Todd runs full speed after it with kids cheering him on. It reminds Todd of a play the Cubs made last night and he says, "Hey, did you see that play Sammy Sosa made last night?" Mostly boys nod agreement.

Kids continue arriving, some from tennis, soccer and pom pon practice, many still in uniform. Like clockwork, people begin moving to the pavilion a little after 5:30. Lynne, the Student-to-Student/CROYA Encounters (STS) staff member (See Chapter Seven), arrives just in time with a four-foot sandwich from Subway. Kids begin opening bags of chips and cans of soda, then dig into the sub. Lynne remembered to order it half-veggie, since two of the CROYA boys are vegetarian. There's eating, talking and general teenage goofing around while everyone eats. This is typically how a CROYA meeting begins. There's always social time and food—often it's pizza, but as Todd explains later, they'll try for variety for the executive committee meetings.

Most are juniors or seniors and have been involved with CROYA for a while. Now, they're on the High School Executive Committee, the youth leaders who are responsible for making things happen. The air is charged with excitement this evening for the first meeting of the school year. Kids are still catching up on summer activities with one another, the weather has turned cooler, and individual members are anticipating their new leadership roles at CROYA.

Aashish, this year's executive committee chairman, begins the meeting by handing out plastic purple CROYA visors. They're corny but the kids get into the spirit, putting the visors on—sometimes upside down—amid the din. Aashish capitalizes on the energy, suggesting they all wear their visors to school on the day of the first Wednesday Youth Committee meeting, which will be next week. He explains that it will send a message to people, about the executive committee's commitment and cohesion. Chris, a senior and very outgoing, breaks in, "No way—we'll get beat up!" But he laughs and everyone knows he's kidding. Besides, he's the one wearing his visor like a tiara. They all seem generally happy to have received this gift, and someone suggests they each wear a CROYA tee shirt that day too. And so it is agreed. This will be a way of generating some public relations for CROYA as they start the year, and hopefully sparking the interest of new students.

Next comes the icebreaker for the evening: Todd hands green balloons to everyone and tells them to blow them up as big as possible. Then he instructs them to get a partner, preferably someone they don't know well, and move outside the pavilion. Everyone complies with lots of jokes and laughter. Outside, Todd explains that the object is for each team to burst the balloon between their bodies without using their hands. Pairs begin wedging the balloons between their torsos or their bottoms. It's harder than they thought! A few are successful and are rewarded with applause and cheers. Then a group of four or five form a line, with a balloon between each of them. They look like a giant caterpillar as they begin to move back and forth trying to break the balloons. After a few seconds, they fall apart laughing without having broken a single balloon.

Icebreaker number two is a sing-along. Jamie and Aashish stand on a picnic table to lead the song, explaining that it is a "repeat after me" song, which is met with groans and good-natured comments. The song goes something like,

"I said a boom chicka boom ...
I said a boom chicka boom ...
I said a boom, chicka rocka, chicka rocka, chicka boom!"

They do several verses, varying it with "hillbilly" style, "baby" style and finally CROYA style. Everyone joins in with real enthusiasm. None of the "I'm too cool to do this" attitude often found with teenagers is present here, though one girl does complain that she has sung this song "a million times since she was little." Lynne, a CROYA staff member, reminds her, "So what? It's still fun!" It becomes clear that one of tonight's objectives is to impress upon the executive committee that to a large extent they set the tone at CROYA. Other members will look to them for leadership, so if members of the executive committee don't join in ice-breakers and games, or if they talk and cause distractions at meetings, other kids at CROYA will do the same.

Icebreakers are an integral part of CROYA programs, and they work, getting people who don't know one another very well to interact, and loosening inhibitions. (See Chapter Ten.)

It's now time for a quick group picture, then on to business. Picture taking is another common occurrence at CROYA: Staff offices are covered with photo collages of various events; photo albums line the shelves near the sitting area; and each year a photographer takes a group shot of all the CROYA members, usually outside on some playground equipment.

Back in the pavilion, all members introduce themselves, their position on the committee and the one thing they are most excited about this year. Aashish and Todd go over business, upcoming events, ideas for the Recreation Center open house (including pie eating and Jell-O "snarfing"), and CROYA's Alcohol, Drug and Smoking Policy for Executive Committee Members (see Appendix). This is a serious talk and everyone listens attentively. (See Chapter Four.)

The meeting wraps up with Aashish suggesting the executive committee members socialize together more often outside CROYA events—have dinner, go to movies, have sleep-overs—and all heartily agree. Before they go, Todd asks each person to make one or two posters advertising the first Youth Committee meeting. The posters will be hung in high school all this week. Kids break up into groups and get busy with poster board and colorful markers.

Elections

Being a member of the "Committee of Twenty," a name by which the executive committee is sometimes called, is a leadership position similar to student council in the high school. Students must express interest in running, meet certain criteria, and make brief speeches on election night. This is one of the more serious CROYA meetings, as nervous students prepare at different levels for their presentations. Some write formal speeches while others talk spontaneously. Elections are held over two weekly youth meetings in the spring, since there are so many positions and CROYA staff want to give each candidate ample time to speak.

The election process, in a nutshell:

- **Interested students declare their candidacy to either the senior high youth worker or any other staff member. This is done at least a week in advance. Exceptions are made closer to elections for those positions that may be unopposed or for those students who are unsure until the last day.**
- **CROYA staff speaks to each candidate individually to make sure that they understand the responsibilities each position entails, that they are able to commit the time and effort, and that CROYA's policy on drugs and alcohol will hold them to a high standard.**
- **Ballots are printed (See sample below) and photocopied.**
- **On election night, each candidate makes a brief one- to three-minute speech about his or her desire to hold a position, typically talking about their qualifications and previous experience, and what CROYA has meant to them.**
- **CROYA staff hand out one ballot to each person attending, then collect the ballots for tally that same night. Note: Youth interested in voting but unable to attend that meeting can stop into a staff member's office the hour before the meeting begins to cast their "absentee" votes, or see the senior high youth worker at school.**
- **Immediately following the meeting, CROYA staff manually tally the votes and then call each student to report election results, and spend as much time as youth need to talk about feelings and possible disappointments. No students are involved in the ballot process (other than to cast their votes) in order to assure the integrity of the elections.**

There are other criteria for certain positions as well. For example, the candidates need to be juniors (for one of the STS vice-chairs), or seniors (for the position of chairperson). The gender of "Parliamentarians" needs to be balanced—one male and one female—to be politically correct during certain initiations that take place. (See Appendix for Executive Committee Requirements.)

Those who do not win in the first round of elections, which are for the chair, vice chair, STS chair, and STS co-vice chairs, are encouraged by CROYA staff to run for a different position at the next meeting. Since these young people are generally most involved in CROYA and sincerely interested in being on the executive committee, staff goes out of the way to show youth their value to CROYA, and encourage them to persevere in the face of adversity.

Also, since the executive committee is held to a higher standard with respect to CROYA's Alcohol, Drug and Smoking Policy, CROYA staff are quick to process incidents involving executive committee members. This entails a meeting with the CROYA youth, who are not shy about voicing their feelings about such incidents.

Sample Election Ballot

CROYA EXECUTIVE COMMITTEE ELECTION BALLOT

Statement to all candidates:

"I understand that by running for the CROYA Executive Committee I may have the opportunity to represent CROYA for the youth of Lake Forest and Lake Bluff. If I am elected, I will uphold the CROYA Drug / Alcohol Policy, and treat myself and others in the 'spirit of CROYA.' I further understand that I represent CROYA when I am participating in a CROYA event as well as outside of CROYA activities in my personal life. In the event that I do not uphold these expectations, I will act in accordance with the stipulations set forth by the CROYA staff."

CHAIR (Circle 1)   **VICE CHAIR (Circle 1)**

Candidate names   Candidate names

STS CHAIR (Circle 1)   **STS CO-VICE CHAIR (Circle 2)**

Candidate names   Candidate names

Senior High Executive Committee Positions and Responsibilities:

The following descriptions of the executive committee positions and responsibilities were written by the CROYA youth holding these positions during the last school year. Annually, they compile a booklet titled, *Everything You Wanted to Know About CROYA but Were Afraid to Ask*, in which they describe in their own words what they do in their respective positions. Their representation of their own responsibilities captures best the essence of CROYA.

Chairperson

As the chairman, I have many responsibilities. Every Monday after school, I meet with Todd to plan the upcoming senior youth meeting that takes place on Wednesday. Together we write up the agenda for the meeting and go over the game we will play with the McPheeter's chairman (See description below). My main responsibility, however, is to lead the youth meetings on Wednesday. On that day, I usually arrive around 4:30 P.M. to go over the agenda. Then I make all the signup sheets that need to go around that night. We use signup sheets for things like upcoming community service projects, decorating for the next dance, or whatever event happens to be coming up at CROYA. At 5:30, the weekly dinner meeting occurs, where pizza and soda are served to everyone who attends. When 7:00 P.M. rolls around, the youth committee begins. As chairman, I lead the meeting and give all the information to the members. My job appears to be very structured and organized, but I really enjoy it and have a great time doing what I do. Being chairman and a member of CROYA has enabled me to meet great people and have a great time. I hope everyone tries it out, and gets involved in all the fun.

— *Aashish Bhansali, Chair*

Vice Chair

The position of vice chairman has proven to be an exciting one. My main responsibility is to plan the youth committee's road trips. These road trips consist of a bunch of kids from CROYA hopping on a bus and traveling to fun and crazy places, like a haunted house or the I-MAX Theater. However, being vice chairman isn't only about road trips. I must be ready to assist the chairman with anything he or she needs. I must also be ready to run any particular meeting if the chairman can't make it. The vice-chairman's position involves a great deal of responsibility and dedication, but I also feel that it is great fun!

— *Chris Torrance, Vice Chair*

McPheeters Chairs (two people)

As "McPheeters," our job on the executive committee is to make up and plan the weekly game for the Wednesday night senior youth meetings. Our challenge is to think up new and creative games each week, like "What's Behind That Door," the "Photo Scavenger Hunt" and "Singled Out." We meet each week with Todd Nahigian, the senior high youth worker, to plan these extraordinary events. Then we run the games after business is conducted at the youth meeting." (See Chapter Ten for game descriptions and "how-to.")

— *Aakash Bhansali and Devin Wall, McPheeters Chairs*

Parliamentarians (two people)

As parliamentarians, it is our duty to make new youth committee members welcome and comfortable through our initiation ritual. (See Chapter Six.) We do this by singling them out, bringing them to the center of attention, and making them do demeaning acts that reduce them to our level. These activities include (but are not limited to) drinking "mystery juice," jumping through hoops, proposing marriage to our chairman and so on. Another aspect of our job is to keep everyone attentive and in line during the youth meetings. One strategy for this is to station ourselves and other executive committee members throughout the circle of kids, so that we can "shush" them and act as positive role models.

— *Christie Schmitt and Eric Hachikian, Parliamentarians*

Public Relations Chairs (two people)

Each year, senior-high CROYA puts out a book called *Everything You Wanted to Know about CROYA but Were Afraid to Ask*. This goes out to all incoming freshmen, new students, and curious minds that may not be familiar with or aware of CROYA. It contains the 4-1-1 on all CROYA activities, from dances to playing football with the cops to the inside scoop on all the executive members' jobs. It's our job to write and organize the book, but we seek out other perspectives from CROYA members to write the entries. And, it's full of lots of great CROYA pictures to make it fun to read.

— *Katie Lenz and Liz Denniston, Public Relations Chairs*

Fundraising Chairs (two people)

As fundraising chairs, we have accepted the large responsibility of raising money for the youth committee. Throughout the year, we work closely with the staff to coordinate such fundraising activities as car washes, poinsettia sales, dances, and a rummage sale that have benefited the CROYA organization. The money that we raise is put toward improving the CROYA facility, such as buying new compact discs and electronic equipment. Our role on the executive committee expands our responsibility beyond fundraising, making both of us active participants in the CROYA atmosphere. The 1998–1999 school year has been very successful, and the staff has been very encouraging of our new ideas and contributions. For instance, this is the first time we have attempted a rummage sale during which we earned over $800. In addition, as members of the executive committee we constantly interact with youth committee members. This helps us get to know other people, learn to work together and have more fun.

— *Anne Grossman and Jamie Stone, Fundraising Chairs*

Cable Coordinators (two people)

Being the *CROYA Goes Cable* coordinator chairs is definitely the most universal position on the executive committee. You could almost call us the court jesters of the board, because when we do sit down to write, produce, or edit a show, it's all about fun. The show's main objective is to give information about CROYA, but also to entertain and attract people to CROYA. Each show includes an interview with someone and footage of CROYA events. To make it happen, we first work with the cable host and senior-high youth worker to write a script for the upcoming show. Then we tape it, either at CROYA or on location somewhere. We work closely with the local cable company, Lake Forest TV, to take advantage of their special cameras, editing equipment and expertise. A lot of our non-cable show time is also spent giving advice and help to the other executive committee members on whatever happens to be going on at CROYA.

— *Conor O'Grady and Richard Hoopis, Cable Coordinators*

Cable Host

The prestigious honor of the position of host of our proclaimed cable show is perfect for anyone who loves to frolic in front of a camera as I do. This position requires an enormous amount of creativity and a little bit of copying from people like David Letterman and other such renowned comedy show hosts. We usually start with a big idea, then narrow it down as we write the script. I have had a lot of fun both in writing and hosting the *CROYA Goes Cable* show. We still have a few episodes to film. Who knows what the next show will have me doing? Whatever it is, I am up to the challenge.

— *Josh Rosenthal, Cable Host*

Topic Night Chairpersons (three people)

Our intellectual trio of topic night chairs *extraordinaire* runs periodic discussions over a wide variety of topics concerning teenage issues. In a nutshell, we get together about three times per year to discuss serious, yet interesting matters. Topics we have tackled include teen drug and alcohol problems, eating disorders, sexual relations and much more. Topic night enlightens kids and allows them to express their problems to help youth know that they are not alone. (See Chapter Seven.)

— *Molly Dapier, Dan Guerin, and Tim Juedes, Topic Night Chairs*

Student-to-Student/CROYA Encounters (STS) Chair

Being the STS chair has been rewarding in countless ways. First and foremost, I have had the opportunity to reach out to different members of the community through projects like PADS, Habitat for Humanity, Women's Residential Services, Stepping Stones, and eighth-grade tours. Planning these events is another part of the chairwoman's job. I work closely with Lynne, the STS staff person, to connect with organizations. Once we have field experiences planned, I also work with my vice chairs to organize and get volunteers. We hold monthly STS meetings at the high school and we contact the kids who are interested in helping. As part of my job, I must be comfortable talking in front of large groups of people, both kids and adults. For instance, each year at the Freshman Mixer I make a presentation about STS in front of all the incoming freshmen and parents.

— *Kristina Lazos, STS Chair*

Student-to-Student/CROYA Encounters (STS)

Vice-Chairs (2 people)

Being STS vice-chairwomen is a lot of fun and work! We experience many things through this position. We have been able to lead and participate in many community service projects, help organize, develop and lead many activities with the seniors of our community, and we have had the chance to be peer mentors in the STS/Peer Training Program. (See Chapter Seven.) Regularly, we meet as a team with Lynne, the STS staff person, to discuss and organize upcoming events. Then we circulate signup sheets and monthly STS meetings and at weekly CROYA youth meetings. Prior to field experiences, we get ready by shopping, setting up, and doing things like making centerpieces for our senior rap dinners. This year we came up with new ideas for STS, such as a Valentine's party at Westmoreland Nursing Home and the monthly lunch meetings. We have learned great leadership and organizational skills through this position. Also by being STS Vice Chairwomen, we have had a great opportunity to work with the other executive committee members, the CROYA staff and of course, we have had fun!

— *Laura Szech and Courtney Nyren, STS Vice Chairs*

Poster Board Chair

When I ran for this position, I really didn't know what I was in for, but I so desperately wanted to be on the executive committee that I'd do anything. Being a sophomore on the executive committee is fairly rare. Once I got the job I slowly learned my duties. Every week I make eight to twelve posters announcing CROYA's youth meetings, events and games and hang them up all over the high school. This sounds easier than it really is. It's really fun but time consuming. But I love the position and being on the CROYA executive committee.

— *Meredith Jones, Poster Board Chair*

Student Council Liaison

As Student Council Liaison, it is my job to be the link between CROYA and student council. Each year one of the six student council executives (elected in late spring) is appointed this position. Throughout the year, these two organizations work together to co-sponsor events such as Homecoming, Winter Formal, Turnabout and Spring Fling, (See Chapter Nine) so it is important that both be well informed. The student council liaison attends both the CROYA meeting and the student council meeting each week and extra executive meetings when necessary. This position is not only the key to keeping CROYA and student council on the same page, but it is fun as well. It's a great job to have.

— *Jamie Sayatovic, Student Council Liaison*

☙ Youth Comment on Executive Committee Experience

"People know I'm on "exec." It is important for people our age to feel important, to take on leadership roles. It shows that we're respected. Adults and peers look up to us."

"The "Execs" don't make all the decisions. We brainstorm concepts and then bring them to the weekly youth group meetings for a vote."

"You have to earn your spot on the "exec," it gives you something to strive for."

"It's amazing to feel so respected by so many adults."

"Our opinions are just as important as the staff's."

"When you're on "exec", you help out more."

"Being on "exec" is not as much a job, but a reward, and we enjoy doing it."

Junior High Executive Committee

The Junior High Executive Committee is different from the Senior High committee in several ways: The junior high youth group presently has two smaller executive committees that meet during lunch periods with the junior high youth worker, who goes onsite to the schools to facilitate their meetings and efforts. Their enthusiasm, however, is not to be outdone by the high school kids. By the time students get to seventh-grade, many are eager for the opportunity to attend CROYA meetings and events and become involved in the process.

Junior High Executive Committee Structure and Responsibilities

"It's not only that you're in CROYA, you are CROYA."

— Garrett Skelly,
Deer Path Junior High School eighth-grader

The junior high executive committees are structured differently than the senior high "exec." First, in order to be on the exec, interested junior high students "put their names into a hat" (after learning about responsibilities involved) at a CROYA meeting at the beginning of the school year. Eighth-graders who were on exec in the prior year have the option of staying on. Eight names each are picked for both seventh and eighth grades (or as many as are needed to fill vacant slots) and for each school. Since CROYA serves the Lake Forest, Lake Bluff and Knollwood communities, they want to assure equal representation from each town.

Second, at the junior high, executive committee members act as a committee rather than having individual positions and responsibilities, as the senior group does. CROYA staff is considering moving toward more structure on the committee, with positions and responsibilities. But currently, since there isn't a specific poster person as there is at the high school, all members might make posters for upcoming CROYA events while they meet. Or, when helping make announcements at weekly youth meetings, all executive members present at the meeting share the spotlight. Also, executive committee members have the responsibility of making phone calls reminding fellow CROYA youth of upcoming events and responsibilities, such as bringing baked goods for a bake sale.

Junior high exec meets about two times per month, during their lunch period. The junior high youth worker goes onsite to the schools to make regular meetings possible and easier for kids who are involved in a lot of activities at school and often have a harder time getting rides to CROYA. These meetings are small and students are clearly comfortable with the process and the outcome of their involvement on these executive committees. For the seventh-graders, who have eagerly waited to be a part of CROYA, it is a particular honor to be on "Exec."

When asked about their roles as executive committee members, students talk about having the opportunity to plan events and know about what's going on at CROYA. They see their role as informing others of CROYA programs in order to be seen as leaders and get more of their friends to come to CROYA. They are the "representatives for CROYA," as well as for their classmates, listening to friends' ideas and taking them back to the organization. In conjunction with this, they feel that being part of CROYA means more and that they are more invested because they are on the executive committee.

Deer Path Junior High eighth-grader Shauna McCarthy also makes the point, "Since these are smaller meetings, we're heard more easily." This forum serves to reinforce the CROYA philosophy of being "run by youth." Another eighth-grader observes that he now feels more comfortable when speaking in front of groups as a result of helping to run CROYA meetings. And Caroline Crouch, a Lake Bluff seventh grader sums it up by saying, "You share in something that other people don't have."

The CROYA Adult Board

"CROYA has had, on the board level, a group of people genuinely interested in sustaining CROYA."

— Scott Bermingham, former Adult Board chair

"The Senior Commission is modeling its board after CROYA's adult board."

— Bob Kiely, Lake Forest city manager

CROYA's adult board has undergone changes in structure, purpose, and membership over the years, as has the selection process for board members. The first criterion for board members is that they be somehow connected in the youth world. Consisting of six to eight members, CROYA's board draws from educational, political, and community members as well as city officials, to obtain a diverse set of people dedicated to supporting and preserving CROYA. Not surprisingly, educators such as superintendents, principals, and presidents of local colleges have been among CROYA's most valuable board members and strongest supporters. Not only have they contributed significantly through their professional knowledge and understanding of youth, they have helped provide resources for CROYA. These include their valued individual input, financial resources, use of their facilities, help from faculty and staff, and referrals to people, places and things.

Official board members usually include one representative each from both the middle school (Lake Forest and Lake Bluff) and high school districts (Lake Forest High School), one resident from each community (typically parents), and always includes the youth chair of the senior high youth committee (See Chapter Four). The youth committee chair reports on current CROYA activities and takes information back to the youth committee. While not official board members, the CROYA staff also attends all board meetings to talk about recent events and programs and offer support to the board. Additional board members are added upon discretion of the board. For instance, the president of a local college is currently serving on the board. In the past, mayors, religious leaders, Parks and Recreation Department staff, business leaders and parent representatives of APT's and PTO's have been board members.

The chair of the board is the only person who holds a position with stated responsibilities. Meeting regularly with the CROYA director, the adult board chair helps map out the board's goals and helps CROYA find the resources to realize them. In keeping with CROYA's philosophy and process for working with youth, CROYA's adult board uses the group process approach to decision making. All board meetings are posted and open to the public. Meeting quarterly, members receive a CROYA newsletter and packet two weeks in advance of meetings for preparation. At the first board meeting of the school year, CROYA's newly elected senior high executive committee chair comes to the board meeting to meet the adult board. Then, as needed, young people attend board meetings to make presentations.

An example of a board responsibility includes the decision to commission this book. Once the youth of CROYA had voted to go ahead with the concept of writing a book, the board deliberated objectives for the book, cost, funding, and community perception, and then eventually approved the project.

Attending a board meeting, one is struck by the diversity, genuine interest, and important contributions of the board members. While the adult board has changed significantly over the years, both in terms of functionality and resources (See Chapter Two), it serves CROYA well as the resource board it is today.

5

The CROYA Staff

⚮

"These then are the key elements: Love, commitment, a mission, a vision, and a passion are what create places of hope and draw youth to those places."

— Urban Sanctuaries, Jossey-Bass Publishers[†]

CROYA HAS GROWN OVER THE YEARS, both as an agency and in the number and capacity of its staff. Critical to the ongoing success of CROYA, there are currently five: Director, Senior High Youth Worker, Junior High Youth Worker, Leadership & Life Skills Youth Worker, and a part-time secretary. Potential candidates, when there is a job opening at CROYA, usually possess a bachelor's degree in education, psychology or counseling, or parks and recreation. Ideally they've had some job experience in one of these fields as well.

But CROYA staff are much more than qualifications on paper. They all possess certain essential qualities and skills for their work—commitment, the genuine desire to work with youth, and a tremendous capacity to relate to young adults. Their energy is limitless, even when they work long days that stretch into evenings, as they often do. They are accessible to the youth, via mailboxes in schools, voice mail at CROYA, home phone numbers, and by virtue of their constant presence in the schools. They remember thousands of student names, including the current seventh- through twelfth-graders, in addition to scores of CROYA alumni. Walking down a school hallway with a CROYA staff member goes like this: "Hey, Katie, how's it going? Jodie, I like your new haircut! Jason,

[†] See References, page 160.

how was your round of golf? Melissa, how are you? How did the swim meet go? Josh, call me about the retreat!" Not to mention the genuine smiles, hugs and high fives that go with the territory.

And their warmth and caring is infectious. An important goal of the staff is to gain the trust of the young people of the community so that staff can be there to listen, lend a helping hand, and intervene when necessary. CROYA is a safe place for kids and that's why they keep coming back. Adults here have earned special status with the youth, who think of them not as grownups who are looking to judge or tell them what to do, but as friends, and it takes a special kind of adult to achieve this status.

As with everything else at CROYA, they've honed their staff responsibilities to ensure that things run smoothly. That's why each staff member has a specific job title and responsibilities to go with it. Despite this, staff works closely together, with a lot of overlap in job responsibilities. The "that's not my job" mentality is nowhere to be found at CROYA, and is another critical ingredient in their success. There are always at least two staff members at every CROYA program; all four attend the weekly youth meetings and other major events. Not only are staff eager to help one another whenever needed, they are accessible to school personnel, parents involved in committees concerning youth, or other communities trying to get their own "CROYA's" off the ground.

CROYA Staff Titles and Responsibilities

Director

"It's all about relationship building."

Kamy Daddono, the current director of CROYA, has been a staff member since 1986, providing valuable continuity to the organization. Not only is she "terribly into kids," as former director Margot Martino once put it, Kamy is an excellent manager and effective at interfacing with parents, city officials, and community members.

The title "director" might be somewhat misleading in her case, because she must operate effectively on two different levels: as a director in all that implies, and as a youth worker. As director, she helps facilitate the CROYA adult board, made up of influential and highly respected community leaders. (See Chapter Four.) In addition, Kamy is a member of the City of Lake Forest's Executive Staff Team, made up of city department heads, such as the police chief, executive director of recreation, and director of city finance.

In addition, she is responsible for the budget, staff evaluations and training, building maintenance and more, as any other director would be.

As the critical community liaison for CROYA, the director must also, in her words, "submerge myself in the community" and "be out there." This means representing the agency and the youth within the community, maintaining positive relations with the organization's many constituents, and looking for "natural links" for CROYA to be involved in worthwhile community activities involving young people. On the flip side, she acts as a resource on issues concerning youth. CROYA has come to be the source for such information, looked upon as having the pulse of the kids in this community. In this role as well, the director delivers speeches and presentations about CROYA to such groups as LEAD (Linking Efforts Against Drugs), and APT (Association of Parents and Teachers), and meets with various community groups and organizations. (See Chapter Eleven.)

Despite all this, the director of CROYA doesn't sit in an office wearing a business suit and go home at 5:00 P.M. CROYA's director is an integral part of the real work the agency does with kids. Kamy attends the weekly youth meetings, semiannual weekend retreats, dances, leadership training and countless other CROYA events. She drives and facilitates new endeavors such as the recent commission of this book and the establishment of CROYA's Resource Gallery. Most importantly, Kamy is with and among the youth just like any other staff member, wearing jeans and sitting on the floor, eating pizza and "rapping" with kids, lending an ear, giving advice when asked, seeking help for youths in crisis and, most importantly, having fun.

Leadership and Life Skills (STS) Youth Worker

> *"I've made friends for life. These are the wonderful perks you get working at CROYA."*

Lynne Siegel, known as the Student-to-Student/CROYA Encounters (STS) youth worker, could best be described as the firecracker of the staff. Her personality is vivacious and bursting with energy, and she brings that energy to her job and her relationship with youth. A staff member for seven years, Lynne first spent four years as the junior high youth worker before switching to STS when it became a full-time staff position.

Peer Training

One of Lynne's major STS responsibilities is coordinating and teaching

Peer Training at the high school every fall. (See Chapter Seven.) Working closely with high school staff, she develops a schedule, arranges for CROYA staff and faculty to teach, and then embarks on a campaign to recruit students to the program. This involves posting schedules, holding STS lunch meetings, setting up a booth at the annual club fair in the cafeteria, and campaigning one-on-one with students. Once peer training gets underway, Lynne is at the high school four days per week, teaching five to six classes concurrently for ten weeks. (See Chapter Seven.)

Retreats

In addition, as the STS staff person, Lynne is responsible for planning and executing both the fall and spring retreats. (See Chapter Eight.) This is no small task. Retreat planning begins months before a retreat. Once student retreat leaders are selected, which involves soliciting volunteers and then making careful selections, Lynne begins holding a series of retreat-planning meetings with youth. At these meetings, youth and staff painstakingly plan every detail of the upcoming retreat, from what kind of skits to perform to what games to play and what movie to select. At meetings, young people go over their roles and responsibilities thoroughly, rehearse skits, and prepare individual retreat packets, among other things.

For Lynne, this also means advertising the retreat, sending out letters and permission slips, collecting money, interfacing with parents, arranging for adult chaperones, and keeping organized as the retreat approaches. In addition, she must coordinate with the camp in terms of bed space and food, shop ahead of time for items like water and treats, and remember to bring essentials from CROYA such as flashlights, batteries, and walkie-talkies.

During the retreat weekend, while the student retreat leaders really run the individual segments and groups, Lynne is behind the scenes making sure everything runs smoothly. She interfaces with adult retreat leaders and chaperones, making sure they know what's coming up and what their responsibilities are. She works closely with student retreat leaders, confirming their upcoming parts and making sure everyone stays on schedule. She never stops moving all weekend, with clipboard and water bottle in hand, Lynne really ensures that the organizational part of the retreat moves along smoothly.

STS/CROYA Encounters Field Experiences

Another critical element of the STS staff person's job is coordinating the field experiences. The whole purpose of peer training is to prepare students to participate in these service-oriented projects. Lynne feels passionate about this part of her job, commenting, "I never thought I'd be so service oriented." In coordinating field experiences, Lynne's role is to oversee the process as she works closely with the student STS chair and co-chairs. (See Chapter Four.) They are the liaisons with the agencies with whom CROYA works, such as Public Action to Deliver Shelter (P.A.D.S.) and Stepping Stones. (See Chapter Seven.) They arrange for what service CROYA might perform, when they will do it, and how many students they'll need. They then recruit students who are interested in working on those field experiences, arrange for supplies if need be, and coordinate rides and carpooling when they go to places such as P.A.D.S. There is also specific pre-training involved for many of these field experiences. For instance, Stepping Stones comes onsite to CROYA once or twice a year to conduct training for youth. When CROYA youth go to P.A.D.S., a homeless shelter, Lynne will conduct a pre-talk about what to expect and what youth's role will be at the shelter.

Meeting with the student STS chair and co-chairs regularly, they help plan and coordinate field experiences such as the eighth-grade presentations with the junior high youth worker. They also hold monthly lunch meetings in the school to communicate STS news and events. CROYA alternates STS meeting locations depending on the youth involved. They alternate between lunch meetings and evening meetings at CROYA, depending on which attracts more kids at any given time. As Lynne says, "STS youth are not necessarily always CROYA youth," and they need to be sensitive to that. Sometimes, STS students are more apt to attend meetings at school rather than coming to CROYA. Monthly STS meetings at the high school have been very successful this year. This is yet another example of CROYA staff's ability to adjust situations to meet the needs of youth, experimenting until they find the right method.

Relationship Building and Outreach

In addition to all this, Lynne goes into the high school every week, touching base with school staff and youth. She often has lunch with individual students or groups, just to socialize or sometimes to talk to a student in trouble. This year, at the request of a group of young women from a peer training class, she agreed to meet with them weekly for lunch, just to keep the good thing they had going. They talk about girl stuff—purses, guys, TV shows—whatever comes up. And Lynne loves it. In her words, "I like to be *in*." It's a testament to her that *the girls* requested they keep meeting.

Lynne also spends a good deal of time networking with current and new agencies with which CROYA works. She recently had a woman from Stepping Stones come in to make a presentation to youth. CROYA was already involved with them, but the meeting sparked new interest among students, many of whom signed up that evening to do the volunteer work with children in hospitals. (See Chapter Seven.) Also, Lynne is always looking for new opportunities for interesting and worthwhile field experiences.

The STS youth worker plays a vital role in the life of CROYA, making possible a well-developed service arm in an already busy youth agency.

Senior High Youth Worker

> *"I love what I do and am rewarded by it every day. Getting up in the morning and coming here is a happy thing. I take it for granted. But once in a while we sit around as a staff and appreciate what we do. On Wednesday nights, I take stock in what we do."*

Todd Nahigian exudes warmth from the moment you meet him, with a big smile for everyone he encounters.

A member of CROYA's staff for five years as senior high youth worker, Todd entered CROYA at a time of staff expansion. Formerly, the senior high youth worker was also responsible for the STS/Peer Training program. Now there are two staff members to cover those responsibilities, and as Todd explains, "I don't think this position, or STS, could be what it is today if we hadn't created two separate positions." This is not hard to believe once Todd explains all that he does.

Relationship Building and Outreach

As the senior high youth worker, Todd is responsible for, in his words, "Networking with kids, getting into their world, finding out what makes them tick. Whether it's a kid in trouble or one who's doing great, they have something to gain here. Also, building self-esteem. Even if a kid is using drugs or drinking, and we, as a staff, may or may not know that, they don't have to feel judged at CROYA. We treat everyone the same."

Todd spends an average of three days per week in the high school (including all day every Wednesday, the day of the senior youth committee meeting), hanging posters, making CROYA announcements, talking to a teacher or a dean, seeking out kids involved in an upcoming program or simply connecting with executive committee members. Todd explains, "You always find kids who have something to tell you, someone who wants to share a story." Being in the high school allows him the flexibility to have lunch with the kids spontaneously and develop relationships even further.

In addition, he is CROYA's student council liaison, working closely with school student council members and the student council body to keep the relationship between CROYA and the high school strong and productive. (See Chapter Eleven.) Annual activities that are co-sponsored by CROYA and the student council are the three annual dances, the Freshman Mixer, homecoming weekend, and Spring Fling. (See Chapters Seven and Nine.)

Todd also sits on many boards in the community as the CROYA representative, having an influence and representing CROYA youth. For example, he works with the board of the Beanery, which is run by The Volunteer Bureau. Its board is also made up of young people and uses a "CROYA"-like process.

Weekly Senior High Youth Meetings, Programs and Events

Todd explains that the "every kid is important" philosophy is "paramount to CROYA's success." He goes on to say, "When a kid walks in the door, the energy in our greeting is critical. They walk in this door and they feel good. They are accepted. They can be who they are."

One of Todd's biggest responsibilities is facilitating the senior high executive committee and weekly senior high youth meetings. (See Chapters Four and Six.) Todd's challenge is to keep all the kids on a committee of twenty invested. As he explains, "Without the executive committee to foster ideas and enthusiasm, we wouldn't have anything to talk about at our weekly youth meetings." In this role, Todd also meets weekly with the executive committee chairperson to plan the meeting and determine what work needs to be done. Depending on what's going on that particular week, he might also meet with individual committee members such as the cable crew to write the script for the next show, or the McPheeters chairmen to plan this week's game. This part of the job is challenging and ongoing. While the executive committee is made up of and run by youth, Todd is a key player in the process.

Other responsibilities of the senior high youth worker include coordinating programs and events such as community service projects, dances, concerts, the annual Donut Bowl with the police, and outings like baseball games and bowling. (See Chapters Seven and Nine.)

Facilitation and The CROYA Process

Delegation is also critical in Todd's job. An important ingredient of

CROYA's success hinges on the fact that it is the young who are driving the process, not the adults, so there is a delicate balance in helping kids stay on track without running the show. And, as Todd explains, "Part of the process of delegating to youth is that things fall through the cracks."

Over time, CROYA staff has learned how to help young people avoid this without stepping in and doing all the work. For instance, in preparation for a CROYA event, Todd might make one phone call to an exec member, who will in turn call the other exec members to remind them of their responsibilities. And, in delegation, Todd clarifies, "We, as adults need to appreciate the level at which *they* (the kids) do it. Their perceived success is not necessarily the same as *our* perceived success." This again ties into the CROYA philosophy of a youth-driven program that is run by youth, and evaluated on their terms.

This is not to say that CROYA staff don't step in and circumvent problems or offer guidance when necessary. For example, when youth are producing something that represents CROYA, like a booklet or a ticket design for an upcoming dance, the staff must ensure that the piece is appropriate and somewhat professional. When the CROYA name is featured as a sponsor or co-sponsor of an event, it's up to the staff to ensure that CROYA youth give the right impression.

Counseling

Another aspect of Todd's and other CROYA staff responsibilities is helping youths who may be in trouble. If there is a problem or behavior that's dangerous, he is there to help. Whether that means talking to the youth one-on-one, or referring more serious issues to appropriate people who are qualified to help, Todd is sensitive to his responsibility in this area. (See Chapter Twelve.) His and the staff's main objective is to keep kids safe and to help them in any way they can. Todd revels in this aspect of his job, saying, "I am a role model for the youth here. I like the idea of helping kids grow up to be healthy, to be good."

Daily, Todd's office is filled with kids meeting about upcoming programs or just wanting to rap. On one such day, while another meeting was taking place and Todd happened to be out of the building, some boys dropped by after school, asking, "Where's Todd?" They hung out in his office waiting for him, shooting hoops with a Styrofoam ball and coming out occasionally to ask, "Is Todd coming back soon?" By virtue of the larger number of students in high school and their level of independence (they often drive and have more say in what they do with their time), every minute of Todd's time seems filled with CROYA activities.

Junior High Youth Worker

"If you could create a perfect job, wouldn't this be it?"

In her second year as junior high youth worker at CROYA, Gretchen Gronau describes her job at CROYA as "multifaceted" in that "no two things are alike." She explains that since she interacts with youth in school and out, her job and her relationship with youth "reflect life." And since she works with seventh- and eighth-graders who are "in transition" between being young kids and high school students, with the types of activities and responsibilities that entails, she needs a particular sensitivity. She describes these students as "easier to pull in" to programs and events, but at the same time "more skeptical." She clarifies, "They are so conscious about what other people think about their choices."

Attending a junior high youth meeting, one would notice the difference from the senior youth meetings. Junior high students are visibly struggling with adolescence. There are groups of boys, for instance, who cannot seem to keep still or quiet for even an instant. They toss candy, tell private jokes and giggle, and congregate in their safe groups. Other boys and girls, while not much different in age, seem vastly more mature at times, taking leadership roles and acting more mature. Some seventh-graders are still very small, waiting for their growth spurts to bring them up to par, while others look several years older because of their size. And all junior high students seem to be constantly bursting with energy.

It takes skill, energy, and good humor to harness this energy to help young people drive their own programs. Gretchen is skilled at communicating and eliciting information and ideas from kids, keeping them on track and making it fun before their attention span is exhausted. At times she seems like a big kid herself, talking to kids about fashion and taking a 500-mile bike ride along with CROYA youth. Her genuine enthusiasm and fun-loving nature blend well with this group.

Junior High Youth Meetings, Programs and Events

Like the senior high youth worker, the junior high youth worker is responsible for, among other things, facilitating the biweekly junior high youth meetings, which take place about every other Tuesday from 5:00–6:00 P.M. at CROYA. She also holds occasional youth meetings at the Lake Bluff middle school and at the private schools in the community, depending on what is going on and what is the best way to connect with the most kids.

In addition, she oversees the junior high executive committees.

Unlike the senior high executive committee, who meet at the CROYA facility, Gretchen goes onsite for meetings at each middle school twice a month and each private school once a month. Their executive committees are smaller, with four to five students on each. Meeting at lunchtime, Gretchen starts in the cafeteria, reminding members of the meeting and leading them to a designated classroom to eat and meet, with her providing pizza or dessert.(See Chapter Four.)

Gretchen oversees and facilitates all junior high special events, including ice and roller skating and cosmic bowling. CROYA also sponsors three junior high dances each year: a back to school dance, Hollyball, and a spring dance. They hold parties at CROYA for Halloween, Christmas and Hanukkah, St. Valentine's Day and St. Patrick's Day. After major events such as Hollyball, Gretchen distributes feedback forms to find out what kids liked, what they didn't, and what they'd do differently next time. This information proves valuable during the planning of next year's programs.

Other responsibilities of the junior high youth worker include coordinating CROYA's Most Excellent Adventure (See Chapter Eight), Girls Night Out (See Chapter Seven), and any other annual or one-time programs or events involving the junior high students.

Community Service Projects

Additionally, Gretchen works with junior high youth on service projects approximately once a month. These include the annual Christmas Character Brunch, packing lunches for the P.A.D.S. shelter, adopting a family at Christmas with Catholic Charities, and helping in a soup kitchen. (See Chapter Seven.) Occasionally, they'll have a bake sale to raise money in connection with one of these programs, such as for purchasing food for the P.A.D.S. lunches.

In addition to bake sales, junior high students hold an annual end-of-summer car wash and sell poinsettias along with the senior youth committees for fundraising efforts. This year, two junior high students were among the top four poinsettia salespeople, which was no small achievement. Coming in number two and three, they sold $944 and $851 in poinsettias respectively, and each earned cash prizes. (See Chapter Fourteen.)

Counseling

Like all CROYA staff, Gretchen is responsible for identifying youths at risk who may need intervention from parents and/or professional counseling. Many young people today struggle with issues such as eating disorders, sexuality, depression, suicidal thoughts, and substance abuse. As the adult closest to this group of students, she needs to be alert to times when the seriousness of such matters might exceed the parameters of her role at CROYA, and know when and to whom to make outreach efforts. (See Chapter Twelve.)

Parent Liaison

In connection with this, another role of CROYA staff is to interface with parents. Such interactions are usually initiated by parents who are concerned about their children or who want to commend the CROYA staff for something they've done. For example, one parent called Gretchen to ask her advice. In conjunction with a CROYA program, the parent's son was involved with another boy whom she thought "questionable," a perception largely based on the boy's appearance. Gretchen was able to tell the mother about CROYA's experience with the boy and to assure her that staff would be sensitive to her concerns. CROYA staff is able to view kids in a larger context, being aware of their lives in and out of school and at CROYA. They also know that appearances, which may include body piercing and drug references on clothing, are not necessarily indications of "bad" or "troubled" kids. Young people want to be noticed and to differentiate themselves from others. Staff knows this and can act as a sounding board for parents concerned about their children. They are also prepared to deal with indications that a kid is in trouble and needs help.

Another mother called after the poinsettia fundraiser this year. While prizes were originally to be awarded to the top four salespeople, two students had each sold over $500 in poinsettias this year. CROYA acknowledged these two with gift certificates from the local chamber of commerce. The mother let Gretchen know how much this meant to her son.

Occasionally, though, CROYA staff will have to decide whether to call parents about a problem that has occurred during a CROYA program. The staff's first and foremost objective is to preserve the trust they have with both the youth and the parents, while keeping kids safe and making them accountable when necessary. It's a delicate process, because young people who come to CROYA often do so because, among other things, they don't feel scrutinized and judged there as they might at home or at school. CROYA staff doesn't want to become additional authority figures attempting to keep kids "in line." Generally, kids respect that. As Gretchen says, "CROYA is very protective of the kids." But staff will hold youth accountable, sometimes calling parents, when their behavior at a CROYA program warrants it.

Secretary

> *"The way in which the staff interacts with each other is an extension of the way they work with kids. It's very supportive, a very warm and caring environment."*

Barbara Sugars describes her position at CROYA as more "behind the scenes," but CROYA staff describes her as the "ultimate keeper of the staff." Before CROYA had a secretary, the staff got bogged down in a lot of administrative details that limited their time with youth. Barbara answers the phones, handles most correspondence and communications pieces, pays the bills, assists the director with the budget, and takes care of time cards, office supplies, and food orders. She is also responsible for the CROYA database, the Teenage Placement Service (see Chapter Seven) and the annual poinsettia fundraiser. More, she has become integral to the staff's relationship-building with youth and community, providing continuity and information when the staff is in the field working with youth and the community.

CROYA's Database and Communications

One of Barbara's priorities during her first year was to further develop the CROYA database. Given the large number of programs, events, meetings, subgroups, youth and community groups that CROYA serves, having a well-organized database has improved CROYA's efficiency and communication. Every month, for example, Barbara sends out the calendars to CROYA youth, city officials, community groups and others on their mailing list. She can produce separate labels for those receiving the junior high calendar and the senior high calendar. If a special meeting of a subgroup is coming up, such as STS or the executive committee, she can extract the names of just those involved students to whom to send a flyer or letter. Her efforts have paid off, as evidenced by the ease and frequency with which CROYA sends out communications. (See Chapter Thirteen.)

CROYA's mailings include monthly calendars, flyers for special events and meetings, meeting reminder cards, a quarterly newsletter, tickets and programs for events, and annual booklets. Barbara helps in these endeavors, not only with her computer and word processing know-how, but with her creative input that gives that flyer, for instance, a little extra pizzazz.

Teenage Placement Service (TAPS)

As TAPS coordinator, Barbara interacts with students and community members, acting as the gatekeeper for applications and job postings. While it is the responsibility of students to check the job bulletin board and pursue opportunities on their own, Barbara will sometimes call a student when she hears of a job for which they are well suited, or when she knows someone is particularly eager to earn money. (See Chapter Seven.)

Annual Fundraiser

Barbara is also instrumental in making the annual poinsettia fundraiser a success. She works with other staff members, meets with the local supplier to choose plants and determine prices, and sends letters to everyone who bought poinsettias during the previous year. After designing the poinsettia sales packets, she works with students to assemble hundreds of packets for distribution. Finally, she manages the database when orders come in. This is a challenge because young people don't always remember to whom they sold plants. To solve this dilemma, Barbara creates two lists—one by purchaser and one by salesperson—to make pickup and delivery run smoothly. She also collects and keeps track of money coming in and helps organize and sort poinsettias. (See Chapter Thirteen.)

Ꮿ Youth Comment on CROYA Staff

"It has a lot to do with the staff. They always suggest things. If they weren't here, I don't know how we would get things done. They can even be like our peers, helping us brainstorm ideas on everything from games to programs."

"They're younger and still know what's cool."

"The staff are a big part of encouraging attendance at CROYA meetings—walking around the cafeteria, saying hi, talking up CROYA."

"It's great the way they are always around at school, the beach, wherever."

"The staff knows when to laugh it off and when to set us straight."

"They treat us like a friend who cares."

"They are goofy."

"They eat junk food like we do."

"They are so honest and straight up."

"Even if they don't know you, there is someone you can turn to."

"CROYA adapts to different groups of kids. They're constantly changing to meet the needs of the kids."

Youth Involvement

As with everything else, it isn't trademark CROYA if young people aren't involved in the process. This goes for the staff hiring procedure as well. Once youth worker applicants have been narrowed to two by the staff, CROYA youth are given the opportunity to interview each applicant at a special youth meeting. They then vote on their choice for the new staff member. Given that every staff member works so closely with the youth, it is critical to have youth "buy in," and they take this job very seriously. Flyers are sent out to everyone on CROYA's mailing list. (See Chapter Thirteen.)

A typical notice in a CROYA flyer:
HEY STUDENTS! WE NEED YOUR HELP!

We want you to come to CROYA on
Thursday, October 1, 5:15–7:30 P.M.
To help interview the candidates
for the Junior High Youth Worker position.
Your input is very important.
Pizza will be served.

About fifty youths attend this interview meeting, which is run like other meetings—"CROYA-style." Sitting on the floor with food, drinks and candy, one candidate joins the circle as students take turns questioning the interviewee on some conventional and not-so-conventional topics. The following are sample questions asked by youth at an interview for Junior High Youth Worker:

- **How long have you been interested in working with kids and why?**
- **What event has changed you as a person?**
- **What was the most daring thing you've ever done?**
- **What do you think you'll be doing ten years from now?**
- **What gets on your nerves?**
- **What was your most embarrassing experience?**
- **What are you most proud of having done in your life?**
- **If you had the opportunity to be famous, would you take that job or this job?**
- **What's your favorite movie and book?**
- **What personality trait do you like about yourself most, and why?**
- **Are you a Cubs fan?**
- **In a conversation, do you tend to talk more or listen more?**
- **Do you smoke or drink?**

- If you could have dinner with any person, dead or alive, who would it be?
- If you were stuck on a deserted island and you could only bring three things, what would you bring?
- How would you handle being here alone with all these kids?
- How would you describe a good friend, and what does a good friend mean to you?
- When was the last time you cried in front of someone?

After answering these questions for about forty-five minutes, the interviewee is asked to leave so that CROYA staff and youth can discuss their impressions of that person. As usual, CROYA youth are not afraid to say how they feel.

Youth Impressions of One Candidate:
- Adorable
- Nice
- Seemed like a CROYA person
- Loosened up when things got funny
- Very personable
- Seemed very qualified
- Not afraid to admit stuff
- Seemed like she didn't just want the job for money
- Answered all of our questions
- Never chose to pass on a question
- Confident, open and honest
- More experience with kids than the other applicant
- Outgoing

The second candidate then comes in and the process is repeated. After processing all this information "CROYA-style," youth vote for the candidate of their choice. Their standard procedure is to pass around small pieces of paper, have students write their votes and then put them into a bowl. Later, the CROYA staff tallies the votes, and then take students' choice into consideration when making the final selection. One can see why CROYA youth feel entirely part of the process and that their voices matter in everything, from what kind of pop and candy they like, to who will work at CROYA as *their* youth worker.

Sample CROYA Job Posting:

Career Opportunity
Youth Worker
Committee Representing Our Young Adults (CROYA)

Work with administrators in all schools, public and private, in Lake Forest and Lake Bluff. CROYA is the youth committee funded by The City of Lake Forest and the Village of Lake Bluff.

- **Activities include working evenings and some weekends.**
- **Must be flexible enough to work with both junior and senior high school groups.**
- **Attend all retreats and overnights.**

Must be able to recognize signals that might indicate that a student has a problem:

- **Youth worker will discuss these signs with the staff for guidance on how to handle this problem.**
- **Will work with the CROYA staff to provide psychological referral.**

Requires BA/BS degree in Education, Recreation, Psychology or a related field.

Salary Range: $28,900-$40,000

This is your chance to become a member of a select and vital team.

Apply by (Date) to:
The City of Lake Forest
Equal Opportunity Employer

Chaperones

Sometimes taken for granted, chaperones are a rare breed of people who support CROYA in an extremely important function. They are used and needed to manage and assure the safety of larger groups of young people during programs and events outside the CROYA facility, such as retreats, outings, dances, or at any time when the number of CROYA staff is insufficient (approximately one adult to ten youth). These are the people who go on sleepless retreat weekends, stand around at dances for hours, and listen to heavy metal music during rock concerts. And they seem to love every minute of it. Being around CROYA is infectious for adults who are "into" kids. The reward is in the hugs, familiarity and general acceptance from youth, and from the feeling that they are giving back.

CROYA's chaperones range from teachers and recreation department staff to CROYA alumni and college students. They are often young people in their mid-to-late twenties who work with youth in some capacity. They are loyal and have become familiar to the kids, which is important. Chaperones serve as adult leaders during retreat weekends, when youth often reveal very private things about themselves. They are sometimes called upon to make difficult decisions regarding accountability for actions. They are always charged with being enthusiastic and energetic as they interact with youth.

CROYA pays chaperones a competitive wage for their time, in addition to whatever food and lodging go along with the event. While they've got a list of regular chaperones, they use the two local colleges for additional help when needed, especially for dances. Posting flyers always brings the chaperones they need.

Shelley Taylor, an elementary school teacher who has been chaperoning CROYA events for years, does it for several reasons. A friend of one CROYA staff member, she began chaperoning as a favor and a way of making a little extra money. But she got hooked. Now she says she likes being an example for young people, of someone who has "been where they are" and has turned out okay. She likes the feeling of "giving back" and she genuinely enjoys CROYA kids and events.

It is important to keep in mind that in working with youth, chaperones do not always have the same knowledge base as staff. Additional training is sometimes needed, and provided by CROYA, for programs such as retreat weekends. Furthermore, parents of CROYA youth are *not* asked to chaperone CROYA events. This is to ensure that youth perceive CROYA as a sacred place. The CROYA staff serves as surrogate adults, whom young people come to trust, respect, and rely upon for adult guidance. And CROYA youth want to feel uninhibited during programs and events.

6

Weekly Youth Meetings

Cℛℰℴⅅ

"I never have a bigger smile than when I walk through the doors of CROYA and see everybody there."

— Chris Torrance, 1998–99 CROYA
executive committee vice-chair

Weekly youth meetings are the core of CROYA's work with young people. Anyone in grades seven or eight (for junior high meetings) and grades nine through twelve (for senior high meetings) can attend. As stressed earlier, there is no membership as such in CROYA. Teen residents of Lake Forest, Lake Bluff, and Knollwood are free to attend as many or as few CROYA meetings and events as they wish. Key elements of the weekly meetings are their regularity and predictability in scheduling and format. Occasionally, it will be announced that a weekly youth meeting will have a special purpose, such as a Topic Night or Jell-O wrestling. (See Chapters Seven and Nine.) But for most meetings throughout the year, the descriptions below apply. The important elements are that the youth have come to know what to expect and are comfortable just showing up. Since they occur mid-week, the meetings are a welcome break from school, other activities, and homework.

Junior High Youth Meetings

Biweekly Junior Youth Meeting Sample Agenda
5:00 Junior High Youth Worker begins the meeting
- Start with an icebreaker in which everyone participates.

• Conduct business (e.g., upcoming events, meetings, community service projects)—what needs to be done, signups, etc.
5:40 Game time; just for fun. (See Chapter Ten.)
6:00 Meeting ends – hang out until about 6:15 p.m.
(Times vary based on objectives for the meeting)

Taking place approximately every two weeks, the junior high meetings resemble senior high meetings in structure only. Seventh- and eighth-graders bring their own set of adolescent characteristics and idiosyncrasies to bear on what is sure to be a lively hour. On one such night in early spring, a mixture of spring fever and first-day-back-from-spring-break excitement combine for a spirited meeting during which no one can stop talking.

After some pre-meeting social time, Gretchen, the junior high youth worker, attempts to quiet the group now seated on the carpeted floor. An icebreaker entitled "What did you like about spring break?" takes a long time to complete with the forty-odd youths in attendance. Each time someone tells what they liked about spring break, individuals bursting with news of their own begin talking to people nearby. For instance, when one young girl says she liked getting tan, everyone else in the circle begins talking excitedly about their experiences with sun and tanning during the past week. There are also some smaller groups sitting together, seemingly unable to focus on the larger purpose at hand, whose constant side conversations add to the din.

Gretchen exhibits Herculean patience; an adult in different circumstances might scream or make threats to bring some order to the chaos. She restores order again and again as they finish the icebreaker and she plows through the short list of announcements and things to do. At times other CROYA staff members, who have strategically placed themselves throughout the circle, chime in to help quiet the kids, using their own individual styles and methods. And this does work, with different youths responding to a variety of cues and authority figures.

Somehow, by around 5:40 P.M., Gretchen manages to have talked about upcoming events and dates and circulate signups for community service projects and subcommittees. Normally, youngsters would be a part of this process, but since this meeting is right after spring break, Gretchen runs it. Then, with some relief and a tremendous release of pent-up energy and excitement, staff and youth burst forth into the spring evening for a much-needed game of Spud on the field outside.

While this meeting may differ from other junior high youth meetings in that youth are particularly restless on this day, the objectives, format, and youth are the same. Junior high students have a lot of energy, enthusiasm and, at times, difficulty restraining themselves in large group situations. CROYA staff know this and have structured meetings accordingly, keeping the business time as brief as possible and making sure there is ample opportunity for physical adolescent hormonal release. Sometimes, the staff simply "throws in the towel" and postpones business until another time, doing a couple of quick announcements and then letting the kids have fun.

While meetings are purposeful and integral to CROYA's successful programming, staff is sensitive to the mood and needs of youth. Sometimes staff abandons the meeting agenda when they sense that going forward would be counterproductive. Ultimately, objectives are met and much is accomplished over the course of a school year. At the end of this meeting, for example, signup sheets are filled and students have taken whatever forms and dates they need for upcoming events. They've seen their friends, expended post-school-day energy and, most importantly, had fun. And for some weekly youth meetings, the agenda is a party. Every year, CROYA hosts a Halloween party, a holiday party in December and a Valentine's Day party, on nights when youth meetings would occur.

While the weekly youth meeting is the cornerstone of CROYA, the formula is so simple that one might wonder what all the fuss is about. But CROYA is much more complex than this, with extensive programming and ongoing relationship building that result from twenty years of working with the youth of Lake Forest, Lake Bluff and Knollwood.

Junior High Subcommittee Planning Meetings

Subcommittee meetings are also an integral part of the CROYA process for working with youth. These are different and separate from the biweekly youth meetings, and are usually scheduled during lunches or after school. For virtually every event that CROYA plans, young people are involved in the process. This means that they ask for volunteers to work on subcommittees that help plan events, such as dances, holiday parties, CROYA's Most Excellent Adventure, and the Girls Summer Extravaganza. Once again, any youth interested in helping on a committee will have the opportunity. Subcommittee members discuss everything from what kind of food to serve to game preferences and prizes. CROYA staff brings in past program evaluations to share and use in planning repeat events.

Kids who attended previous events also give feedback on their experiences, and recommend changes. For some events or programs, such as the Lake County Races volunteer effort, the names of one or more committee chairs will be chosen out of a hat. For some students this is their first opportunity to hold a leadership position. All meetings are working meetings and youth are given additional responsibilities, such as planning skits or making and assembling packets for upcoming programs.

Senior High Youth Meetings

Weekly Senior Youth Meeting Sample Agenda
7:00 Youth Committee Chairman begins the meeting
- Introduction of new members, with humorous initiations. Award of candy or some small prize.
- Business (e.g., upcoming programs, events, and community service projects)—what's happening, what needs to be done.

7:40 McPheeters Chairs lead in a game. (See Chapter Ten.)
8:00 Meeting ends—hang out until 9:00 P.M. or later.

By the time high school youth are on the CROYA executive committee and leading weekly youth meetings, they are comfortable before groups and in using The CROYA Process. (See Chapter Three.) The chair of the executive committee really runs the weekly senior high youth meeting, with the help of the vice-chair, the senior high youth worker, CROYA youth who have contributions to make, and the rest of the CROYA staff. The senior high youth worker adjusts his role depending on the needs of youth, with variables such as mood, preoccupation, or various teen issues affecting involvement. While it is important to give the youth chair responsibility and room to exercise his or her leadership abilities, flexibility is also critical, sensing the youth chair's mood and ability to lead on any given day. All meetings begin with some funny method of quieting the socializing youth and bringing everybody together for the business portion of the gathering.

Group Attention-getting Technique
The chair says very loudly, "If you can hear my voice, clap once!" (clapping once). "If you can hear my voice, clap twice!" (clapping twice). "If you can hear my voice, clap three times!" (clapping three times). These chants are done in rapid succession, serving to grab attention and get the kids to engage in an activity meant to create order.

With young people sitting in a loose circle on the large rug or on the couches just beyond, they get down to business. The chairperson and other members of the youth group, such as subcommittee chairs, will:

- **Perform funny initiations on new CROYA kids (See this chapter for more details). This also serves as an icebreaker of sorts, since the size of the weekly youth meetings prohibits the traditional icebreaker where each attendee is asked to respond. (See Chapter Ten.)**
- **Make announcements about upcoming CROYA events, such as dances, retreats, elections, and Student to Student (STS) field service projects. (See Chapters Seven and Nine.)**
- **Pass around signup forms for committees and community service projects, such as United Way Labeling, Friends of Lake Forest Library Book Sale, etc. (See chapter Seven.)**
- **Solicit input from youth in attendance, feedback on events that have just occurred, ideas for upcoming events, or hot topics and incidents occurring at the schools.**
- **Announce job openings through the CROYA Teenage Placement Service. (TAPS—See Chapter Seven.)**
- **Vote on important issues, such as what tee shirt designs to use, which youth worker to hire, or whether to embark on a book-writing project for CROYA.**

Once business is conducted (thirty–forty minutes), the McPheeters chairpersons lead the group in a fun and often raucous game. Sometimes it's indoors, others outside, but kids are always up for a good time. In addition, they need the energy release after a day of school and anticipation of homework to be done later that evening. (See Chapter Ten for game ideas and resources.)

CROYA youth meetings end with some "hangout" time in the facility. The stereo is turned on, youth workers talk and work with youngsters on upcoming programs or events, and the kids enjoy a bit more social time before heading home. Often, a core group will hang out until ten or eleven o'clock. Staff is flexible in this area, recognizing this as an important opportunity to be accessible to kids who just need to talk or may have a problem to discuss. In addition, often a group of kids will go somewhere for post-CROYA get-togethers, going to the town beach or to get something to eat.

ℭℨ Youth Comment on Why They Come to CROYA Meetings

"It's the middle of the week – break day!"

"I get to hang out with students I don't normally hang out with at school."

"A mid-week pulse check – if you will."

"I always feel so appreciated for just showing up."

"I love the fact that the staff knows everyone's names."

"A place to de-stress."

"A place to feel important."

"The outrageous fun games!"

"The overall good feeling."

"Not being around my parents. Not doing my homework. Free Food. A chance to get away from everyone and see the staff."

"The girls."

"The boys."

High School Dinner Meetings

Subcommittees meet weekly, to provide input and do the planning and organization involved in making programs and activities happen. Like any board, the executive committees and special planning committees, with help from CROYA staff members, do the lion's share of the work. Committee chairs and vice-chairs work closely with the senior high youth worker to plan and lead meetings that are purposeful and productive.

To this end, the subcommittees meet on Wednesdays for what are called "dinner meetings." They start at 5:30 P.M. with pizza, pasta, or hero sandwiches. Students come from sports practice or other after-school activities, or from home, promptly helping themselves to whatever's on the menu while socializing with peers and CROYA staff. Meetings start soon after, with students sitting on the big rug while eating.

These dinner meetings usually have a specific agenda, announced earlier on the monthly CROYA calendar (e.g., "Retreat Planning Meeting" or "Battle of the Bands Dinner Meeting"). During a Homecoming Dance dinner meeting, for example, the committee begins planning details of the approaching homecoming weekend. The senior high youth worker takes a greater role in facilitating this meeting, having thought through items that need to be addressed, and he keeps members on task and moving along. Reminding students of what was done at last year's dance, he informs them of changes that are in effect this year.

For this year's homecoming, Todd, the senior high youth worker, announces that there will be a greater focus on discouraging alcohol consumption. Also, they need to decide on music, decorations, and refreshments. Then he informs the students that the school and the city have announced that there will be no bonfires and no student drivers in this year's parade, so the group needs to think of other fun alternatives to fill the gaps. Lastly, he reminds everyone rather strongly, "This is *your* homecoming," and that they need to take ownership in putting it together, and not expect the staff to do all the work.

CROYA staff is skilled at this kind of discipline. They know that kids are kids; they need to be reigned in at times, reminded often, and kept on track. But the difference in hearing this from a staff person is that CROYA staff has earned the trust and respect of the young people, the result being that they don't meet with the same resistance to authority that other adults might. They spend a lot more time giving positive reinforcement and letting kids be kids than being authority figures. They know when it's appropriate to be a friend, hang out, and let someone make mistakes, and when taking a stronger stance is necessary. And when they do have to get a little tough, young people respect them.

CROYA youth are accustomed to the dinner meeting process. What ensues is a session of putting forward ideas, discussing them and coming to consensus. Students are clearly angry about the bonfire rule, expressing feelings like, "Any town that won't let a bunch of high schoolers have a bonfire stinks!" Todd gives them room to vent, eventually bringing it back around to the positive, "Let's talk about what we *can* do." Eventually, decisions are made pertaining to big issues, smaller subcommittees are formed to work on things like decorations and refreshments, and follow-up meetings are planned.

It takes anywhere from one to four planning meetings to make dances, concerts, and retreats a reality. Meeting frequency depends on the event and is directly related to the amount of youth involvement on the day of the program or event. Only one meeting is needed prior to a dance, to solicit youth input on things like theme and decorations, because youth don't actually work at a dance; the CROYA staff and school faculty make it happen while students enjoy themselves. On the other hand, for big events such as retreats and Battle of the Bands, meetings are held more often, and not always at dinnertime. For these programs, young people are an integral part of the entire process, from planning to running the actual program. They might meet after school and in the evenings as the event approaches and last-minute details need to be firmed up. Subcommittee planning meetings are an essential element of The CROYA Process. (See Chapter Three.)

☙ Youth Comment on Dinner Meetings

"Dinner meetings are where most of the brainstorming is done. It's a forum for ideas. Anyone can come. It's more interactive than the bigger meetings."

"We can vote on stuff that's going on."

"We give input for other people too – like our friends and people we know at school."

"There don't have to be a lot of people there to get things done."

Food

"CROYA = Calories "R" Our Year-Long Activity"
— Frank Farwell, former mayor of Lake Forest

CROYA youth have been known to say, "CROYA is food." When reminiscing, CROYA alumni often comment on the great food. Early memorandums from former CROYA director Margot Martino noted in 1985, "For some reason food seems to be a necessary ingredient to the youth committee meeting atmosphere. I've brought pretzels and my popcorn popper the last two meetings and the tension between the different groups has lessened." And later, in 1986, "The youth committee have even appointed a food chairman to inform me what they want at each meeting. How can such a small thing do so much?"

Today, food is central to every CROYA meeting and event. This is important to CROYA youth. *Very Important.* Enjoying pizza, candy and junk food (as well as fruits and salads) with friends and staff is a nurturing and bonding experience that really is a critical ingredient in working successfully with youth. When planning programs and events, a lot of discussion centers on what kind of food to have—bagels, pizza, pasta, salads, ice cream sundaes, cookies, and novelty junk food. CROYA youth have very definite opinions about what they want to eat, and discussing the menu has become a CROYA ritual.

☙ Youth Comment on the Importance of FOOD

"It helps. It's an added incentive to come to CROYA."

"There's nothing like sharing a meal with your buddies."

"Food makes it more social. Meetings can still be fun."

"Food and music—what else do you need?"

Friendly Initiations

While technically called "initiations," this ritual is just CROYA's goofy, fun and safe way of welcoming new kids, and sometimes adults, to the CROYA community. While often embarrassing, they are never cruel or dangerous, and no one is ever forced to participate in order to be a part of CROYA. Here are some ideas:

- **Mix up some famous 'mystery juice" with safe (but often gross) combinations of ingredients from the kitchen.**
- **Dance like a chicken or a monkey in the center of the circle with music playing loudly.**
- **Put two tortilla chips or potato chips in your mouth and quack like a duck.**
- **Push an egg across the floor with your nose.**
- **Perform a "stupid human trick' that is unique to you, such as hyper-extending limbs, doing flips into splits, or twisting your tongue so that it looks like a clover.**
- **Share your best pickup line with the youth committee.**
- **Dive through moving "Hula Hoops" so that they keep moving after you're done.**

Staff leaves initiations up to the young people, who are naturally creative and come up with their own crazy and entertaining ideas.

✄ Youth Comment on Their Initiations

"I had to dance like a chicken in the middle of the room!"

"All the seniors were here. It was dead silent, and I had to stand up and tell everyone what I do alone in the dark. I said 'I sleep!'"

"When I was finished with my initiation, they tossed me a goodie bag fill with not only candy, but a list of all the CROYA staff and their phone numbers. I was impressed with how the group welcomed me."

"It's a fun way to start the meetings."

"I try to bring a "new" friend every week just to watch them go through initiations."

"The group cheers you on."

"It's your 15 seconds of fame!"

7

CROYA Programs

"Community and school support, patience, listening carefully to kids, and a physical structure are key."

— Gene Brooke, former
Lake Forest High School counselor

CROYA PROGRAMS IN PLACE today are integral parts of its structure, having been developed, revised, and expanded over the years. Some have stood the test of time, while others—such as Mam'selles, a girls' modeling program—were discontinued when it was deemed they were no longer in sync with CROYA's values and mission. Most of the following programs are considered core programs, i.e., next to the weekly youth meetings and youth committees they are at the heart of CROYA's work with youth.

It's important to stress that while CROYA has become fluent in successful programming, it is the *process* by which these programs come about that is the key element in working with youth. Margot Martino, CROYA's first director, noted in 1986, "We perceive the activities as a vehicle and not an end result." Community leaders and parents often felt that creating more activities for youth was the answer—a mindset that was difficult to overcome in the early days. It wasn't until CROYA came around and the staff began involving youth in the process, from idea to inception, that young people became invested in the programs. Youngsters began to take pride and ownership in deciding on and planning events that *they* wanted.

For most CROYA events, students staff the planning subcommittees and one chair or two co-chair positions. CROYA staff members are always a part of the entire process, helping to facilitate meetings as youth brainstorm and come to consensus on such decisions as what games to play and what food to have. (See Chapters Three and Six.)

Peer Training / Service

Student-to-Student / CROYA Encounters
Peer Training and Field Experiences

Walking into any high school cafeteria at lunchtime is a proceed-at-your-own-risk proposition. The rush for lines, vending machines, microwaves, and social time with peers is fast, loud and intimidating for anyone unfamiliar with the terrain. But for ten weeks every fall at Lake Forest High, something very different and serious is going on in various rooms throughout the school. During one lunch period each week, groups of about ten students, one STS facilitator and usually one peer mentor participate in peer training, formally known as Student-to-Student/CROYA Encounters peer training.

Based on the knowledge that young people often turn to each other to discuss issues and problems before going to adults, the *CROYA Peer Training Manual* states, "The Peer Training program is intended to help teenagers become more skilled in their ability to understand themselves and others better, to listen and respond to themselves and others in healthy ways, and to improve their problem solving abilities in an attempt to be helpful to themselves and to their peers."

Co-sponsored by the high school and CROYA, this program is an example of an excellent partnership between teachers, administrators, and CROYA staff. Despite the fact that it is an elective class for students, who don't receive credits or grades for completing the training, the program's popularity and reputation speak to its success. Upon completion, students become eligible to participate in field experiences in and out of school. Approximately 150 students go through Peer Training for the first time each year. While not graded, students are expected to attend all sessions, with one freebie missed class and the opportunity to make up one other absence. This is a serious program and CROYA and high school staff are firm about the requirements for "graduation" from peer training.

At a typical peer training session, students straggle in for the first five or ten minutes of the period, lunch bags or trays in hand, and sit in a circle on the floor. Amid the rustling, munching, and trading of chips, candy and apples, the facilitator begins with an icebreaker (See

Chapter Ten), then begins one of the ten lessons in the program.

This is another good example of a program that youth asked for and youth built. Originally called "Close Encounters," it was designed by a young CROYA girl named Margot Klimzack, who thought of the idea during CROYA's first retreat in 1987. Later, the high school wanted to be a part of the program and worked with CROYA to integrate it into the school. The *CROYA Peer Training Manual* was revised in the early 1990s by former Lake Forest High School counselor Gene Brooke and CROYA director Kamy Daddono, but remains loyal to the program's original objectives.

Lessons introduce strategies for students to interact better with one another, resolve conflicts and facilitate groups. A session on being a "good helper," for instance, stresses unconditional positive regard, empathy, and being genuine when listening to a friend with a problem. Like all CROYA programs, the success hinges on dialogue among participants, and students are open and honest in sharing.

At the end of each lesson, the facilitator assigns a "Personal Application" for the week. This asks students to apply in their own lives what they have learned in this week's session. For example, after the session on "The Basics of Helping," which talks about unconditional positive regard and attending skills, students are assigned the following personal application from the *CROYA Peer Training Manual*:

> At least once this week, focus on your attending behavior when you are with someone. Pay attention to how you feel and how the other person reacts. The facilitator will then ask students about their experiences this week during next week's session.

During the final peer training session, students graduate and are given a prevention referral card that lists numbers such as Planned Parenthood, Child Abuse Hotline, and Alcoholics Anonymous as a resource for themselves, friends and family. They are now also qualified to participate in STS field experiences. (See list below.)

The STS chairs also hold periodic larger STS meetings during lunch periods at the high school or in the evenings at CROYA, to discuss upcoming field experiences or recruit new students for upcoming peer training classes. A flyer is sent in advance to peer-trained students. On the day of the meetings, the STS staff person and STS chairs round up peer-trained students in the hallways and cafeteria and remind them of the meeting. They offer dessert as an incentive and promise to keep it short. Often, the high school STS faculty member attends as well. Ideally, one of the STS student chairs leads the meeting, giving an overview of upcoming field experiences and passing around signup sheets.

Sample STS Field Experiences

Like everything at CROYA, field experiences evolve over time. Changes are made depending on student interest and community need.

Catholic Charities

STS/CROYA adopts a family for the holidays in conjunction with the Focus Program at the high school. Peer helpers are involved in choosing a family, soliciting donation gifts for the family's "wish list," and planning a party that takes place at CROYA's facility. Last year's adopted family members were victims of a drunk driving accident that resulted in tremendous medical bills. The young boy wished for a battery powered jeep car, and another young boy from Lake Forest and his family donated his "previously owned" car.

CROYA's Most Excellent Adventure

Led by high school students, this one-day event is for junior high students. (See Chapter Eight.)

Habitat for Humanity

When needed, peer helpers join others in putting the finishing touches on new homes built by this organization. This includes yard work, cementing sidewalks, roofing sheds or whatever is needed. Student Caitlin Gorand wrote in the STS CROYA Encounters booklet, *"Though our hands got tired and cold, our hearts were warmed by the fact that we were partaking in such a good deed. Simply knowing that all of our hard work would change the life of a family in need brightened our day."*

Inspiration Cafe

Peer helpers serve and eat dinner with Chicago homeless people.

Junior High Presentations

Peer-trained students make presentations to eighth-graders about topics such as the transition into high school and activities of interest to students.

Lake County Pads (Public Action to Deliver Shelter)

Homeless Shelters

Peer helpers provide fellowship for the homeless: playing cards, talking, and singing Christmas carols at the holidays.

Leadership Training

Peer-trained students and student council members work together to conduct leadership training for junior high students. (See this chapter.)

Peer Mentoring

Peer-trained high school students act as student teachers/mentors in peer training classes.

Retreats

Semi-annual self-exploratory excursions. (See Chapter Eight.)

Senior Citizens Rap Group

Peer helpers hold rap sessions with different groups from the community. For example, for the first time this year, CROYA invited seniors for dinner, dessert and talk at the local community center. During last year's holiday season, CROYA staff and peer helpers prepared dinner (lasagna, bread and salad), made turkey centerpieces for each table (using apples, toothpicks, marshmallows, etc.), and brought homemade desserts. Peer helpers mixed at each table, chatting about anything from school to apartheid. After dinner, everyone sat in a big circle, and young and old shared stories of holiday traditions and the differences in the generations. Some of the seniors told stories of what dating was like "back then," and all involved thoroughly enjoyed the evening.

Stepping Stones

New to STS this year, this field experience is coordinated by Stepping Stones, whose staff trains youth to work with children in hospitals. Using a kit that is provided by the agency, young people go into pediatrics wards of area hospitals to play with the sick children.

Student Council Leadership Program

Annually, peer-trained and student council students lead an afternoon workshop with junior high students on how to be the best leaders they can be.

Tours for Eighth-graders

Peer helpers lead tours during spring visits. This is a favorite among peer helpers. (See Chapter Seven.)

Peer Tutors

Peer-trained students tutor other students, including special needs students, in various subjects. Interested students sign up at STS lunch meetings, specifying their areas of interest and availability. A high school faculty member coordinates the program.

Women's Residential Services

Peer helpers plan and host an annual Halloween party, including stories, face painting and treats for children living at the center. This is a home for substance abuse mothers and their children.

Westmoreland Holiday Party

Peer helpers visit a local nursing home at the holidays, singing Christmas carols, playing "Angel Bingo" and bringing holiday cookies and desserts to share. The seniors particularly enjoy the Angel Bingo. On Valentine's Day, peer helpers go back with carnations and treats in hand, walking through the facility with Valentine's greetings for all.

Community Service Projects

"Youth learn a great deal about themselves when they give of themselves. It's a way to boost self-worth."

— Kamy Daddono, CROYA director

Organizations throughout Lake Forest, Lake Bluff and neighboring communities often need people power to perform tasks ranging from loading books to serving food at local events. CROYA youth help out regularly in these community service projects (also known as CSP's), which support a good cause and provide a chance to be with friends and meet people. Although it is sometimes hard work, it's always fun. Students sign up in advance and receive a CROYA tee shirt for working. The following are some of the regular CSP's CROYA is involved in, with a brief description of the way in which youth volunteer:

Baby Alumni at Lake Forest Hospital—Youth help run an annual carnival for children born at Lake Forest Hospital. This includes face painting, unloading strollers from buses and helping mothers with children.

Catholic Charities—CROYA adopts three families (one for each youth group), asking youth and families to purchase gifts from the wish lists as charitable contributions. Staff organizes the effort and delivers the gifts.

The Harbor—New this year, youth visited a home for people suffering from HIV and/or AIDS. They held a cereal drive, prepared dinner, and spent time socializing with residents. In the spring, they also helped during the home's one-year garden-planting ceremony, greeting people, handing out assignments and serving food.

Holiday Character Brunch—Youth dress in costume and help with games, circulate during brunch and serve as Santa's elves at this annual fundraiser, hosted by Lake Forest and Lake Bluff Junior Women's Club.

Holiday Tree Lighting Ceremony—Once in a while, a CROYA youth is asked to flip the switch, turning on the lights all over Market Square.

Lake County Races—Every April, CROYA youth help sort over 2,000 runners' bags by number in a cordoned-off area on the Lake Bluff Village Green. As chilled incoming runners approach, youth quickly retrieve their bags for them so they can change into dry clothes.

LEAD (Taste of Lake Forest Spaghetti Dinner)—Young people help serve dinner, clear tables, and work at booths.

Friends of the Lake Forest Library Book Sale—CROYA youth clean up after this annual book sale, boxing and loading unsold books onto trucks.

Mrs. Allen—Youth periodically visit the donor of funds to build the CROYA facility.

P.A.D.S. lunches—CROYA supplies bread and lunchmeats while parents donate chips, juice and cookies. Youth pack lunches and drop off at PADS (Public Action to Deliver Shelter), a local shelter for homeless people.

Parent University—Youth act as hall and classroom monitors and work in the babysitting room during this one-day seminar for community members.

Soup Kitchen—Youth check people in, serve food and clean up at a local church.

United Way Labeling—Early in the school year, youth help affix labels to thousands of mailers during the United Way's big fall drive.

Leadership Training

Several times a year, CROYA facilitates various leadership programs for youth. One, a yearly student council leadership program, includes peer-trained high school students (also student council members) who facilitate leadership training for junior high students at the CROYA facility. Working in small groups, this is totally planned and run by young people, with high school students teaching the skills necessary to lead groups and be effective on student council. Youth noticeably gain more from their high school peers than from adults, so staff is careful to stay out of the way and let them do the job.

This opportunity is important for both the senior high as well as the junior high kids. It offers each participant the opportunity to be a leader and a learner. It demonstrates to students that their community efforts are appreciated and respected, and creates sensitivity and awareness of different leadership styles and the importance of diversity.

CROYA also supports schools and community groups in their efforts. Many of these programs—often day-long events held on weekends—are sponsored by local parent/teacher organizations (e.g., APT's and PTO's), who come to CROYA for youth input, facilitator assistance, and help in "talking it up" among kids. CROYA acts as a bridge, helping youth and adults come together to participate in something worthwhile.

Offshoot Programs

These programs are good examples of the opportunity that exists for changing paradigms as a result of CROYA's work with youth and the community. CROYA staff helped develop projects that were entirely youth initiated.

GNO (Girls Night Out)

GNO was formed following CROYA's Most Excellent Adventure several years ago. A group of then-seventh-grade girls, concerned about a friend who they thought might have an eating disorder, asked CROYA staff to provide a forum for discussing issues important to adolescent girls. Meeting once a month, they talk about everything from boyfriends and school to problems with friends. CROYA female staff members attend all meetings, acting as friends and facilitators. This is an excellent example of CROYA's willingness to create programs to "meet youth needs as perceived by youth."

"It's a Girl Thing" Girls Summer Extravaganza

Inspired by the GNO girls last year, CROYA organized a girl's summer program. Consisting of seven events taking place throughout the summer, the girls helped plan and then attended programs of interest to them. This pilot was so successful that male youth have requested their own program for next summer. This year's program included:

Nutrition Day—educational and fun day culminating in cooking a nutritious meal at CROYA.

Pamper Yourself—including relaxation techniques, skin care and makeovers, nails, and hair by professionals in those fields.

Career Day—with local women involved in politics, journalism, and the arts engaging the girls in hands-on learning experiences.

Get Physical—featuring wall climbing, biking, swimming, and a local tri-athlete.

Girls Day Downtown—city road trip to downtown Chicago, including a boat tour of the city, lunch and shopping.

Jelly Belly Tour—tour of a nearby candy factory, with free jelly beans and lunch afterwards.

Grand Finale Sleepover at CROYA—with movie, ice cream, and girl talk followed by a sunrise breakfast at Lake Forest Beach. This afforded the opportunity for connecting and supporting friendship and awareness the girls have developed, and is a good example of youth supporting youth.

Resource Gallery

The Resource Gallery is a place where youth can go to access information on issues such as self-mutilation, body piercing, anxiety disorders, stress, learning disabilities, cancer, and many more. They can do this via the online computer dedicated to the center (confidential and restricted to appropriate sites), or through the hundreds of brochures and books that line the gallery walls. Converted from existing space within the CROYA facility, this nook includes brochure racks, a computer, artwork by teens, and comfortable Crazy Creek chairs that make it a welcome place to read in private, away from curious eyes of librarians, parents, or teachers. The "gallery" aspect features teen artwork, giving artistic outlet to young people who want to express through art the emotional ups and downs of teenage life.

What is even more significant about the Resource Gallery, however, is how it came to be. Two CROYA girls, who had overcome struggles with serious personal issues, expressed the need for accessible, confidential information about their own and other types of issues facing teens. CROYA staff listened to the girls and asked for their involvement in the process of figuring out what to do. This is a good example of CROYA's ability, and the community's readiness, to help youth realize their visions. Working closely with the CROYA director for most of the school year, the girls clarified their vision for a resource gallery and were involved in fundraising and other efforts to make it a reality.

CROYA approached several not-for-profit groups in the community for financial and other assistance. The Friends of the Lake Forest Library responded by donating $2,000 for resources such as brochures and books. The Lake Forest Library donated a computer, and the Lake Forest Hospital Patient Education Center helped design the setup. CROYA was able to pull together an additional $1,000 to purchase information racks and chairs.

Also, in the effort to keep it current and active, CROYA has given responsibility for the Resource Gallery to the public relations chair on the youth executive committee. That person has responsibility for monthly advertising, highlighting a different teen issue each month at a youth meeting, and providing handouts. In addition, they will make presentations along with CROYA staff to various student groups, creating awareness of the gallery as a resource for all youth as well as an artistic venue.

Signature CROYA Programs

CROYA Goes Cable

Two to four times a year, the senior high youth worker and cable chairs write, direct, perform in, and produce a real cable television show. The program, whose objective is to educate the community about CROYA, airs weekly on the local cable network in Lake Forest & Lake Bluff. Its primary purpose is to give viewers a taste of CROYA from their homes, as an inducement to come to CROYA, and to update young people on upcoming events. But for youth, the real reason seems to be "just for the fun of it." It affords students involved a chance to be behind the scenes from the ground up in a television production. And while this is definitely a low-budget and relatively simple format, it's an impressive undertaking.

A typical cable show might, for example, feature an interview with a new CROYA staff member, but this is not your typical interview. The cable host, chosen for his or her outgoing and zany nature, generally does a "Saturday Night Live"-type act, possibly while wearing a goofy hat and sunglasses, and playing jokes on the interviewee. And his co-host acts as a sort of side kick doing something funny, such as nonchalantly reading a book entitled *The New Teenage Body*, the title of which is visible to the audience. Usually filmed in the CROYA facility, extraneous people stroll through, creating interruptions and adding to the act throughout the program. Sometimes these are planned as part of the show; other times they happen spontaneously.

The other half of the show features a recent event at CROYA. One such show entitled "A Day in the Life of a CROYA Kid," begins with footage from Disco Night at CROYA. Kids in seventies attire dance to the song, "Disco Inferno" with the lyrics "Burn, baby, burn." And many CROYA youth are not shy, goofing off in front of the camera and having fun. Another cable show featured Karaoke Night at CROYA. During editing, cable technicians added bylines identifying the different groups singing, such as "freshman girls" and "executive committee."

It's yet another facet of CROYA programming that sets the agency apart. While a lot of work is involved in producing a twenty-minute cable segment, CROYA staff are committed to offering high-level programs that are challenging and fun for the young.

TAPS

The Teenage Placement Service was established in the early days of CROYA in response to one of the original problems identified in the *Youth Needs Assessment* survey. As expressed loudly and clearly by students, that need was for something to do to alleviate the boredom they felt. In short, TAPS is a job networking system to help youth connect with community members for work, with CROYA acting as the go-between. As with many things at CROYA, it has evolved over time. In early days, it was a dominant aspect of CROYA's work. Today, TAPS continues to serve an important role for those youth in need of employment and community members looking for help.

How TAPS works today
- **Kids interested in finding work go to CROYA and fill out job applications.**
- **Community members or local businesses looking for youth for babysitting, yard work, office work, etc., go to CROYA and fill out a card. Cards are color coded by job type (pink–babysitting, green–yard work, lawn care, gray–office, computer work, and yellow–miscellaneous).**

How CROYA youth find out about jobs
- **Incoming jobs are posted on the JOB Bulletin Board at CROYA.**
- **Young people look through the TAPS box where the job cards are kept.**
- **The secretary in charge of TAPS sometimes phones students to match jobs to their skills.**

To avoid liability, CROYA no longer distributes to the community lists of youth interested in work. And while TAPS is not a large part of what CROYA offers, it serves a steady number of young job applicants and residents, with "repeat callers" who use CROYA as their primary source for "help wanted." Summer is the busier season, but during the school year an average of three new job postings per week come into CROYA, and there are always a number of jobs on the board for anyone seeking work.

Topic Night
Senior High Youth Group Topic Night
About three times a year, CROYA hosts what's called "Topic Night" for high school students, during weekly Wednesday youth meetings. On one such night, over 100 kids crowd the CROYA facility to talk about drugs and alcohol. Many are not regular CROYA attendees. Three young people from the community are in recovery, and have come to speak about their experiences with drugs and alcohol. CROYA staff has also arranged to have people from NICASA, (Northern Illinois Council on Alcoholism and Substance Abuse) on hand to answer questions about their prevention and rehabilitation programs and to distribute literature to the interested.

Two of the young speakers are currently Lake Forest High School students; the other participant is a recent graduate. Each takes a turn telling his or her story, which involves an extremely candid discussion of how drug and alcohol addiction has affected their lives.

One young man, who started drinking when he was ten years old, talks about being arrested four times, cutting school frequently, breaking into a local school, vandalizing private property, and running away from home often. The young woman describes feelings of depression and thoughts of suicide. She too ran away a lot and often used her school travel money to buy drugs, which meant she had to "ditch" the train conductors in order to get home. She stresses, "I didn't care about anyone but myself."

The third young man, a CROYA alumnus, works at a retail store while he tries to deal with his addiction through a recovery program and his parents' support. Arrested for driving under the influence (DUI) shortly after high school graduation, his drug and alcohol abuse got so bad that he resorted to searching through medicine chests in people's homes for prescription drugs that had the "right kinds of warning labels,"—those that would get him high. He also talked about taking drugs from strangers and smoking "crack" once because he didn't know what was in the pipe that was handed to him.

All three spent one or more occasions in a treatment center and/or psychiatric hospital in their attempts to get and stay clean. All talked about depression, not wanting to live, not caring about anyone but themselves, and the desire to get high to avoid their feelings. And none believed they had a substance abuse problem until things got so bad that they were faced with life or death choices.

For well over an hour, CROYA youth and additional young people from the community sat silently and listened intently to these stories. They came of their own free will to educate themselves about drugs and alcohol and the reality that young people just like themselves have become addicts. They learned how to spot warning signs in themselves, friends, or family, and they asked questions of the three speakers as well. One asked, "What can we do to support you?" meaning the speakers, to which they replied, "Say hello to us in the hallways at school." Another asked what to do if she felt that a friend might have a problem. The speakers told her to call that person's parents and said that confronting the friend would probably accomplish nothing. Several young adults suggested that parents are part of the problem, because they condone drinking according to their sets of rules, and that our communities still deny that there is a problem. Other students expressed anger at what they perceived as school officials not being more open about these issues. Perhaps adults feel that if they shelter our youth, they can protect them. Youth, however, feel differently. They clearly want to be a part of the dialogue and the solutions.

Toward the end of the meeting, the NICASA representatives spoke briefly about their treatment and prevention programs, explaining that they teach people life skills as part of their recovery from drugs and alcohol. They made themselves available after the meeting and had brought lots of pamphlets for youngsters to take.

After this topic night, a parent of one young man who had attended the program called a CROYA staff member the next morning to commend CROYA for sponsoring the evening. She said that after her son came home, they sat at the kitchen table and had a really open discussion about the very real issues raised. And she asked if CROYA could do more in this area, echoing the sentiment of CROYA youth that more needs to be done.

Other topic night discussions have focused on eating disorders, friends, depression, sex and relationships, and stress. Sometimes they will have speakers—either students from school or expert speakers on certain subjects. On other topic nights, students write down questions and put them into a big bowl as they enter. Then, kids take turns picking, and the whole group discusses that topic. Another variation is to have three main topics, each one discussed in a different room. Students can choose a subject and go to that room to talk about it in a smaller group.

Students know that CROYA provides a safe environment in which to talk about what's on their minds without being judged or censored. They also come for information—for themselves, for friends, for family. They might not use the information today, but the seeds have been planted; knowledge is the first step to discovery, change, and help should they choose to seek it. Confidentiality, respect for others, and the diversity of views is always emphasized at the beginning: "To listen, to share, to take what you want and leave the rest here."

Junior High Youth Group Topic Night

At the end of every school year, the junior high youth group also conducts one topic night just for eighth-graders. The high school students help lead this discussion—a good opportunity for them to model topic night format and behavior. For this occasion, students write questions on paper slips as they come in the door, and put them in a bucket. As they enter CROYA, they see a big sign that reads, "Fill out a piece of paper with a serious question for topic nite, relating to cliques, friend groups, or social issues." A subcommittee made up of junior high youth has met to prepare and to choose general topics for the night, based on what they perceive to be the current pressing issues for kids.

Organized in a circle, next year's senior youth group chairman leads off with some ground rules: "Don't laugh at what people say," and "Keep it confidential—don't spread rumors at lunch tomorrow." The high school leaders also convey the purpose of the night: "To provide a safe and open arena for discussing issues with a large group of your peers. We want you to feel safe and secure in sharing things."

Topics discussed on a recent night include cliques and the shooting incident at Columbine High School in Littleton, Colorado. Eighth-graders are mature and open in their participation, sometimes deferring to high school students whose "modeling" helps pave the way for weighty discussion.

Transitional Activities

"CROYA helps the migration from junior high to high school."

— Community Member

Eighth-Grade Presentations

During the second half of the school year, CROYA, in conjunction with faculty at the middle schools, conducts presentations for eighth-graders on the cusp of becoming high schoolers. Approximately seventeen STS peer-trained high school students lead this program. During the first period of school, eighth-graders go to the school library where high school students sit, lining one side of the library floor. Eighth-graders sit opposite them, with what seems a huge gulf separating them. And to them it is. While the prospect of entering high school is exciting, it comes with fear and anxiety for most students. The high school students they revere now sit opposite them for some one-on-one contact. During one such presentation, Kristina Lazos, a senior at LFHS, tells everyone to move closer to each other before they begin. Eighth-graders and high school students are practically nose to nose before they begin.

Introductions come first, with high schoolers introducing themselves one at a time, saying their grade and what activities they're into. They then break into small groups, three or four high schoolers leading each. As an icebreaker, all the students introduce themselves and say what they are looking forward to in high school. Eighth-graders are obviously somewhat intimidated; they speak very quietly. Their responses range from "activities" to "sports" to "meeting new people."

A bag of questions is then passed around and eighth-graders are told that they'll be rewarded with candy if they ask a question. The questions are posed to the high school students and are designed to help the eighth-graders learn about topics they might not even know to ask about.

Sample Questions

• **Should you go to your locker every period or carry a backpack?**
• **Which teachers and classes do you recommend?**

- **How do I get involved in clubs?**
- **When are finals, and how hard are they?**
- **Are dances fun?**
- **What is athletic study hall?**

Eighth-Grade Tours

Every spring, busloads of eighth-graders walk into the Lake Forest High School auditorium for their first taste of high school. After an introductory session, groups of peer-trained high school students take groups of eighth-graders on tours of the school. These were instituted to give eager and anxious eighth-graders a chance to walk around the high school and to give peer-trained high school students a chance to help out and show off a bit to the soon-to-be freshmen.

This co-curricular program between Lake Forest High School and CROYA requires a lot of planning and coordination. All eighth-graders attend one of three tour dates. Junior high faculty at both public schools (and occasionally the private schools) takes care of special scheduling and buses. The CROYA Student-to-Student (STS) staff member works closely with the high school staff to determine dates and coordinate the schedule for the day. CROYA staff and the high school student assistance coordinator make announcements at STS meetings at the high school, and coordinate signups and scheduling. Each peer-trained high school student is allowed to conduct one tour, during which they are excused from class. They are discouraged from signing up for a tour on any day on which they have a test.

On the day of the tour, high school tour guides arrive at the auditorium ahead of the eighth-graders, to be briefed on expectations and organized into groups. CROYA staff and high school faculty impress upon the students the importance of being positive and not "downing" any aspect of the high school, such as teachers or classes. Students are given a checklist of locations that they are encouraged to visit on their tours.

As eighth-graders arrive, they file into rows of seats, forming the groups that will tour together. Several faculty members, including a dean and a vice principal speak to the eighth-graders. A guidance counselor, for example, tells students that LFHS is a warm, caring place and that most students like it here. He tells them that the counselors and the other faculty want the eighth-graders to like it here too, and encourages them to get involved, to not just go home at 3:10 when school lets out.

Then, several high school students speak to the eighth-graders as well. These include the CROYA student council liaison and STS chair, the current student council president, and a student involved in peer mediation. They each give their own advice to incoming freshmen, ranging from "Get involved" to "Don't be afraid to ask questions."

Then, groups of about ten embark on their journeys through the halls, visiting the cafeteria, nurse's office, outdoor sports fields, and some classrooms. After an hour or so, they reconvene in the cafeteria to chat, using questions provided by CROYA to generate discussion (See Appendix) during refreshments and before returning to buses and classes.

New Student Meeting / Freshman Mixer

In late summer, the new student meeting and freshman mixer are designed to acquaint nervous, excited freshmen and other new students with Lake Forest High. Beginning at around noon, interested students come to CROYA to mix with other kids and staff while having pizza and pop. CROYA upperclassmen are present, greeting students as they walk in and introducing them to others. Staff members engage the group in an icebreaker, asking students to say their names, grades, and how they feel about starting high school. They also play an icebreaker game called "fruit salad" to loosen things up and have some fun.

Dividing by grade level, students board a bus at about one o'clock, and are taken to the high school to meet and hear from school administrators. The principal addresses the students, as do deans and counselors, in an effort to disseminate information and make nervous freshmen feel comfortable. Students then go on a tour of the high school.

Later that same day, students go to the high school for the two-hour freshman mixer that begins at 6:00 P.M. Prior to the start, the CROYA upperclassmen who will help run the mixer show up to get assignments and rehearse skits for the freshmen. Staff gives youth some ideas for skits, such as getting lost in the maze of the high school or using a camp song to put on a funny show. Amazingly, they prepare well in a short period and are ready to perform.

About 100 freshmen assemble in the auditorium. First, there are introductions of the CROYA staff, school administrators such as the assistant principal and a dean, and some officers from CROYA's executive committee and the high school student council. Then the upperclassmen perform the skits they've rehearsed. Dividing into groups, upperclassmen, equipped with a list of questions commonly asked by freshmen, lead the freshmen on extensive tours of the high school before moving outside. The evening culminates in a barbecue—hot dogs and burgers, pop and brownies—accompanied by a student band. Kids and adults linger on the high school lawn, mingling and enjoying one last carefree evening of summer just before school starts.

New Student Lunches

Periodically, the junior high youth worker and STS staff person go into the middle schools to participate in New Student Lunches. Faculty and a couple of current students also participate. Whenever several new students have just entered a school, CROYA tries to make them feel comfortable and give them an overview of some of the things going on.

Pizza and pop are served in a classroom designated for this purpose. CROYA staff takes this opportunity to plug the organization. After introducing themselves and shaking hands, they tell the new students that CROYA is a place to hang out, build floats in the summer, and go on fun trips with other kids. They hand out staff cards with phone numbers, CROYA bumper stickers, and the junior high booklet that talks about a lot of CROYA happenings. They also pass around a signup sheet so they can make sure new students receive the monthly CROYA calendar.

Basically, staff just raps with the new kids, some of whom are more comfortable than others. The STS youth worker might ask, "How's the transition? Do you talk to friends from home?" Later, when she finds out it's one student's very first day, she jokes, "Richard, not a bad way to start! Pizza and pop for lunch!"

End of Year Graduation & Welcome Parties
Eighth-Grade Graduation and Barbecue

Every spring, CROYA hosts an eighth-grade graduation party/welcome to the senior youth committee barbecue. Having been part of CROYA's junior youth committee for two years, eighth-graders now move up to the senior youth committee in a fun graduation-type ceremony. Two balloon arches depict the transition from junior high to high school. Each arch is decorated with symbolic representations of that stage in young people's lives. The junior high arch features flags from the junior high, pictures from CROYA's Most Excellent Adventure (a junior high event), and teenage zits. The high school theme includes dating and pictures from CROYA retreats. Todd, the senior high youth worker at CROYA, often plays the national anthem on his trumpet for an added touch. A junior high band plays outside during the barbecue and there is a raffle drawing for CROYA tee shirts.

Sixth Grade Welcome Party

For the sixth-graders, who are eligible as seventh-graders to be a part of CROYA, there is a Sixth-Grade Welcome party. Members from the junior high youth committee are there to welcome the "rookies" and show off CROYA. Following CROYA youth meeting format, staff and youngsters congregate in a circle to begin the meeting after some social mingling and music. Staff members introduce themselves and then seventh- and eighth-graders speak briefly about different aspects of CROYA that they've been involved in and enjoyed. Staff goes over a calendar of events for summer, encouraging the sixth-graders to join in the fun.

Ice cream cones served by CROYA staff and more social time with new friends follow the meeting.

Recognition Dinner

> *"The Recognition Dinner is an important opportunity to appreciate our successes and thank those adults and youth who have worked so hard in creating the caring culture of CROYA."*

> — Kamy Daddono, CROYA's director

Every spring, as school is winding down and seniors are becoming nostalgic about CROYA and high school, CROYA hosts what it calls the Recognition Dinner. This could best be described as a three-hour celebration where CROYA adults and youth come together to reminisce and give each other "warm fuzzies." The thing that makes this work is the fact that everyone really cares about CROYA and the people involved. It's an opportunity for thank-you's, good-byes, and memories, and comes with lots of genuine tears, laughter, and hugs.

The event requires a lot of planning and preparation, since it involves a catered dinner, invitations, preparation of award certificates and more. Ensuring that the invitation list is thorough is one of the hardest parts. The CROYA Adult Board and the executive committee (both this year's and next year's members-elect) are always invited. And, since this dinner is primarily for graduating seniors, CROYA staff also invites those who have been serving on CROYA subcommittees or coming to lots of youth meetings. There are also additional community leaders to think about—former staff, board members, school personnel, and city officials, for example, are frequently invited.

The evening begins with the Adult Board chair and CROYA staff recognizing, among other people, this year's STS/CROYA Encounters chair and the executive committee chair. Then, the outgoing chairman of the executive committee stands and recognizes the whole "E.C." These speeches are tender, emotion-packed, and straight from the heart. At one point, Aashish, this year's executive committee chairman, tells everyone, "Being on the E.C. has lived up to all my expectations." He asks everyone to come up and "give me a hug" as he says a few words about each member's contributions and awards each a big goofy straw hat as they come up to stand at the front of the room.

Then, this year's executive committee rewards next year's executive committee by passing on certain symbolic and secret joke mementos. For instance, the two McPheeters chairs (games chairmen) pass on their "stud cards," which have been passed along for five years now. The parliamentarians provide incoming members with an initiation starter kit, consisting of zip-lock bags, blindfolds, and a pacifier that has been handed down for years (a symbolic prop meant to keep people quiet at meetings). One female executive member passes on "a candle with which to remember the significance of retreats," and another gives an incoming member a new photo album for future retreat pictures. The CROYA Goes Cable chairs award their successors with a tape of "out-takes" from the upcoming cable show.

Then, the Recognition of Graduating Seniors segment really captures the essence of CROYA: Each senior stands up and briefly tells everyone his or her plans for next year (college or otherwise) and also shares a favorite CROYA memory.

Seniors are each given a certificate by the CROYA staff as well. At this point, Margot Martino, CROYA's first director, reads the two winning senior essays to the whole group. The winners do not know who they are until their essays are read. In these essays, seniors capture beautifully their fondness for CROYA, how its spirit has touched them, and how they feel their experience with the organization has impacted their lives for today and the future.

All the while, adults have sat and listened to the teen jargon, inside jokes, and sometimes-risqué innuendoes typical of healthy adolescents. More than anything, this event conveys the way in which CROYA impacts the lives of these youngsters, who have been so involved during their teen years. It speaks to the dedication, commitment and miraculous work of the CROYA staff and reinforces the significance of this community's support of such an agency. It takes vision, leadership, and faith to stand behind a youth organization that puts control in the hands of youth as CROYA does. This ceremony is an opportunity for all to reflect and be thankful for that. Other communities, struggling to find a way to reach their young people, could use this agency's work as a blueprint for successful youth programming.

☙ Youth Comment
on What They Appreciate About CROYA

"I want to thank the staff of CROYA. Without you, my high school experience would not have been as great."

"CROYA gave me the opportunity to go on a spring retreat with my little sister, who I am very, extremely close to."

"CROYA has been an adventure. It made me who I am and gave me confidence."

"Margot Morrison (former CROYA co-director) once said, 'To pick a favorite CROYA memory is impossible.' Keep CROYA forever."

"CROYA has opened me up to so much more."

"CROYA gives you the confidence and skills to succeed in whatever you choose to do."

"A home away from home."

"Acceptance."

"You don't have to be popular to be a leader."

"Recognition for even the little things you do."

"Gives me the confidence to voice my opinion."

"CROYA is a place to grow as an individual."

"A big family that doesn't make you do laundry."

Scholarship/Senior Essays

Every spring, CROYA awards one $1000 or two $500 scholarships to graduating seniors. Seniors apply by writing a one- to three-page typed senior essay, on the theme "What the Spirit of CROYA Means to Me." Once all essays have been turned in, CROYA staff blocks the writers' names from the essays and prepares a packet of all the essays submitted. These packets are handed out to CROYA youth who want to vote for their favorite essays. The following instructions for voting procedures are included:

> *Dear CROYA Senior Essay Readers:*
> *Please read through all of the essays. Then pick three that stand out as the best representation of what "The Spirit of*

CROYA" means to you.

If you figure out who has written the essays, please do not let that influence which ones you feel are the best.

Rank the three best: 1ˢᵗ, 2ⁿᵈ, 3ʳᵈ.

Call Todd's voice mail (phone #) and vote for 1ˢᵗ, 2ⁿᵈ, 3ʳᵈ.

Please call to vote by Sunday night. If you have and questions, leave me a message and I will call you back.

Thanks for all your help. Todd

Winners of the Senior Essay Contest are announced at the annual Recognition Dinner (See this chapter), during which the essays are read aloud and the winners are awarded their scholarships. (See Appendix for essay requirements and a sample senior essay.)

Financial Aid

Another form of scholarship offered by CROYA is financial assistance for any youth who cannot pay the fee for a special CROYA event or program. While many CROYA programs are free, such as weekly youth meetings and in-house parties, there are charges for some outings, events, and programs such as bowling, retreats, and dances. These often involve the cost of travel or admission to outside facilities. The fees are usually nominal, such as $3—$5.00 for a dance, but are sometimes more, such as $80.00 for a retreat weekend. CROYA puts a note on every program and event flyer offering to absorb the cost if someone cannot pay it (e.g., "Scholarships Available. See CROYA Staff").

While one might expect abuse of this benefit, that is not the case. Students who cannot pay meet with a staff member to request aid. They are then encouraged to repay by contributing time in one of CROYA's community service projects. (See Appendix for Sample Community Service Letter.) As an example, between two and five young people out of the eighty who attend take advantage of this program on retreat weekends.

Sixth-Grade Presentations

Similar to eighth-grade presentations, the junior high executive committees at each middle school make presentations to the sixth-graders about CROYA near the end of the school year. As incoming seventh-graders, this is the first time that sixth-graders are eligible to participate in CROYA, and many have been eagerly awaiting this opportunity. Prior to the presentations, the junior high youth worker works with CROYA youth to put together a booklet about the organization. (See Chapter Thirteen.) This booklet, entitled *CROYA: Who We Are, What We Are, Why We Are—Junior High Booklet 1998–1999*, is kid-friendly and completely authored by youth, with descriptions of different CROYA programs and events, and lots of pictures.

The presentations take place in the gym or the auditorium right at the beginning of the school day or in individual homerooms in larger schools. CROYA staff and youth spread the message, talking about their favorite events and why CROYA is fun. They say things like, "Try it once." "You learn a lot about friendships and how to meet people." "Go to the 70s Cubs game. It is so fun." A good indicator of the interest of sixth-graders is the number of booklets left behind after the presentation—this year there was only one! This also reinforces the notion that encouraging young people to connect and become involved earlier rather than later is key.

☜ Youth Comment on CROYA Programs

"The eighth-grade tour introduces you to high school kids."

"I still see the people who gave me a tour. It just a face to know, but it helps."

"STS is a good way to involve kids who are not active in CROYA. It can be a way to get them "in," or they can just do STS and that's okay too."

"I can't go to everything, but it's nice to have so much to choose from."

"The opportunities are endless."

"You can go to everything or just one program and you still are just as welcomed."

"CROYA lets us do fun and crazy things."

"There's something for everyone."

"TAPS (Teenage Placement Service) is a good thing."

"CROYA is fun, but it is also serious sometimes and you can come to CROYA for help."

"Topic Night is a time when you can say things and people aren't going to go and spread it."

8

Retreats

CㄹA〇

Fall and Spring Weekend Retreats (High School)

"My favorite CROYA memory is of dropping off my daughter for a retreat with her crying and not wanting to go without her friend. Then when I picked her up she said how much she loved the weekend and how she felt so happy."

— Mother of a CROYA youth

IT IS MID-MARCH AT A CAMP in Wisconsin where eighty young people and eight adults embark on their annual spring retreat. CROYA's first retreat was held in the spring 1987 with seventeen youth in attendance. It has earned its waiting list status with young people for good reason. High school students come together here to explore such important issues as school pressures, family, sexuality, and life as a teenager. There are no inhibitions at retreats. From experienced retreat goers and CROYA staff, students learn that this event has the reputation of being safe. To keep it that way, the first page of their retreat package stresses in bold type, **What you say and hear here, stays here.** They are eager to discuss deeply personal things with people they often do not know very well. It turns out to be a memorable, often life-changing experience.

Sample Retreat Flyer
CROYA FALL RETREAT

WHEN: Friday, November 5, — Sunday, November 7. We leave from CROYA (400 Hastings Road, LF) at 4:00PM . We will return to CROYA at 1:00PM on Sunday.

87

WHERE: B'Nai B'rith Beber Camp, Mukwonago, WI.
HOW: We will be traveling by bus.
WHO: Any CROYA youth committee members who have *never* been on a Fall Retreat in the past.

FEE: $80.00, which includes a non-refundable $25.00 deposit. Permission/medical slip authorization form (See Appendix) and deposit are **due by Wednesday, October 27ᵗʰ at the CROYA facility. SPACE IS LIMITED. FIRST COME, FIRST SERVED BASIS.** If we reach our maximum, a waiting list will be started.

    **Scholarships are available.
    For More Information, Contact Lynne, At 615-4307

Friday Night

Retreats begin on Friday afternoon with a raucous hour and a half bus ride north to Wisconsin. On arrival, the students scramble to their respective dorms to claim beds and rooms with friends. After dinner, the first of five large group meetings takes place in the chapel auditorium. The student leaders really run the retreat, and they kick off this evening with a skit they've rehearsed to music and a strobe light. It's quite funny and gets things off to an upbeat start.

Small Group Assignments

Next, group leaders hand out small group assignments. This is done in typical CROYA fashion, with creativity that ensures interaction among everyone from the start. Each person is given a personal retreat packet, the cover of which bears the person's name, hand decorated by the student leaders. Also on the folder appears an action, such as "pat your head" or "make animal noises." Each person must then walk around the room performing that action and looking for other people doing the same thing. This is how each group finds itself in a room filled with eighty-nine people. It's an icebreaker of sorts, forcing everyone to set aside inhibitions among a lot of people they don't know. At another retreat, attendees are given a verse of a song and asked to go around singing it and find the others singing the same song—the people who will be in their small group.

Small Group Icebreakers

Each small group now spends some time together, making introductions and participating in small group icebreakers. In "the human knot," all ten members of a group grasp hands while standing in a circle, and then try to undo the knot without letting go. This forces close physical contact and requires teamwork and ingenuity. No group succeeds this time, but rumor has it that some have escaped the human knot at previous retreats. Or, groups might be asked to rehearse the chorus to a song as they get to know one another, then perform it on the stage for the larger group.

Large Group Kickoff Meeting

Now it's time for some serious business, in which retreat leaders go over the rules and goals for the weekend with the entire group. The retreat leaders have carefully planned this prior to the retreat. Each leader has a part, whether it be reading and explaining goals or explaining how the next event, such as the Telephone Game, is going to work. In each person's retreat packet is a schedule for the weekend, a list of the rules and goals, a list of groups, a story that will be read during the weekend, and some extra paper for taking notes.

Retreat Goals:
- **To create a safe, caring environment in which youth can identify and express their needs.**
- **To establish healthy relationships by maintaining a positive attitude with peers and adult group members.**
- **To provide a sense of wellbeing among members.**
- **To learn more about yourself.**
- **To execute listening and helping skills.**
- **To learn how to give and take positive strokes.**
- **To learn to cooperate.**
- **To make at least one new friend.**
- **To have a blast!**

Retreat Rules:
1. **Everything said here is in complete CONFIDENCE!**
2. **NO DRUGS, ALCOHOL OR TOBACCO ALLOWED!**
3. **Never, ever go anywhere alone. There are BOOGEYMEN out there!**
4. **No leaving the facilities after CURFEW!**
5. **Friday night—lights out at midnight! We have a lot of work to do on Saturday, so we'll need our zzz's.**
6. **Saturday night—be settled by 2:00 A.M.**
7. **When you see/hear the quiet signal (this will be established by the retreat leaders and shared during the first large group session on Friday), close your mouth and open your ears.**

8. **Don't go through other people's belongings.**
9. **Always be respectful of camp property.**
10. **On Sunday morning you must follow the cleanup system and have your room checked out by an adult staff member.**

Large Group Icebreaker: "Who Am I?"

Following this is a large group icebreaker called "Who Am I?" During the rules and goals discussion, retreat leaders have gone around sticking tags on people's backs, with names such as "Michael Jordan," "Madonna" or "Scooby-Doo" written on them. Everyone mills about talking with different people and asking yes-or-no questions to determine who they are. It's another opportunity to meet people in a fun and sometimes frustrating way. After awhile, people who haven't already guessed are told who they are, which is followed by a lot of laughter and discussion of the process.

Movie: Retreat Theme

Kids go to their rooms, bring back their sleeping bags and claim spots all over the floor and sofas of the community room. They help themselves to snacks covering two tables along the wall. Each participant has been asked to contribute a snack for thirty people to the weekend communal reserve. This way, everyone shares in plenty of junk food as well as healthy alternatives like apples and granola bars.

The weekend's theme is now revealed in a movie that everyone watches together. This year's choice, made by the retreat planning committee, is *Say Anything* (Twentieth Century Fox, 1989). As importantly, students have an opportunity to snuggle with eighty other teenagers in a darkened room, pigging out, whispering and giggling over secrets, and gaining momentum for a weekend of learning and fun. This is when everyone begins to settle in and acclimate to a weekend away from family, familiar surroundings, and normal behaviors.

Candle Ceremony

Immediately after the movie, retreat leaders enter the darkened movie room holding candles. Spreading out across the room, each retreat leader takes a turn reading a quote he or she has picked for "Candle Quotes." This is the first retreat for this ceremony and it has an impact. Individual quotes may or may not tie in with the movie, but all are thought provoking and just right to end the first night of the retreat and set the tone for some serious thinking that will take place. Participants also realize that this weekend has been carefully planned and will be full of surprises like this.

Typical Retreat Schedule

Saturday

8:00 A.M. Breakfast

9:00 A.M. Large Group Meeting

- Game
- Read "Warm Fuzzy" story (Confidential)
- Introduction to "Warm Fuzzy" bags (Warm fuzzies are simply nice things that people write to one another on slips of paper. They are a way to reinforce good attributes, giving others "positive strokes." Warm fuzzies are written throughout the weekend and put into individual Warm Fuzzy bags—see below).

10:00 A.M. Small Groups

- Make "Warm Fuzzy" bags (Using small paper lunch bags, small group members sit in their respective break-out rooms with magazines, scissors, glue, and paper bags, creating their own personal "Warm Fuzzy" bags. Each bag turns into a representation of that person and will be used later for storing "Warm Fuzzies.")
- Discussion: "Movie theme"
  - **Which character did you like most/least? Why?**
  - **Which character are you most/least like? Why?**
  - **What theme(s) were revealed? Discuss.**

11:00 A.M. Large Group Meeting

- Discussion about the movie, with some question prompts provided in retreat packets. (Two retreat leaders lead this discussion and, despite the fact that there are 89 people in the room, everyone is quiet and respectful, and a lot of people contribute their thoughts to the discussion.)

11:15 A.M. Headband Activity (See Below)

11:45 A.M. Guided Imagery (See Below)

12:30 P.M. Lunch and Break (During free time until 3:00 P.M., people take walks, play football, rest, or congregate for small discussions, all on the camp's beautiful grounds.)

3:00 P.M. Small Groups

- Interviews in pairs
  - **What do you like the most about yourself?**
  - **If you could have lunch with anyone, dead or alive, who would it be and why?**
  - **If you could choose one day to relive, what day would it be and why?**
- Share meaningful object with group. (Each person has been asked to bring a meaningful object on the retreat. Now is the time when they bring it to small groups and talk about why it's meaningful to them. This is a

surprisingly touching exercise that allows each person to reveal something deeply personal about themselves. One young man brings his guitar pick and talks about how important music is to him, how he expresses himself through it and wants to have a career that involves music.)

• Introduce partner from introductions. (Members tell the small group about their partner, having learned about them in interviews.)

3:45 P.M. Crossing the Line: (A top-secret, large group activity in the gymnasium.)

5:00 P.M. Small Groups

• Ice breaker with group

• "Warm Fuzzy" circle. (In their breakout rooms, groups sit around, taking turns focusing on one person and giving that person verbal warm fuzzies.)

6:30 P.M. Dinner

7:00 P.M. Large Group meeting

• Candle lighting ceremony (Confidential)

7:30 P.M. Small Groups

• Autobiographies/Hot Seat (Now that people know one another better, all are given an opportunity to talk about themselves for a period of time. Again, young people are very open, bringing to the group any issues with which they are struggling and anything about their lives that they feel a burning desire to talk about. This segment takes anywhere from four to six hours.)

Again, confidentiality is critical to the integrity and sacredness of retreats, so not all events can be explained in detail here. Generally, small groups allow for more intimate discussion of planned topics based on the loose themes established with the movie. Large groups give everyone an opportunity to come together, share common trends from small groups, play games, and add variety to the weekend.

Headband Activity

Some of the more serious games in the large group also serve to reinforce aspects of the theme in dramatic ways. For example, late Saturday morning the large group comes together for the "Headband" activity. The retreat leaders are the central players. Each is wearing a headband on which is written in large letters a characteristic such as "class clown." The person wearing the headband does not know what part he or she is playing. The group then engages in a discussion around some specific topic, such as "planning a retreat." They proceed to work together to do just that, and they treat one another according to that other person's characteristic. So, when Laura the "class clown" suggests something, others might shoot down her ideas, saying, "You always make a joke out of everything! Can't you be serious for this?" After about twenty minutes, members try to guess what part they played, and the whole group discusses how our stereotypes affect how we listen to people and how we treat them.

Relaxation and Free Time

Just before lunch on Saturday, CROYA staff leads the large group in guided imagery. First, everyone runs back to their rooms for sleeping bags and pillows, then spreads out on the chapel floor. With background music, CROYA staff reads a story, at intervals instructing participants in relaxation. It's a chance to unwind and get away from some of the serious topics introduced before lunch and afternoon free time. Many of the students fall asleep, while others simply enjoy a rare opportunity to do nothing and simply nurture themselves for twenty minutes.

Serious Business

After free time on Saturday, youth and leaders engage in more small and large group activities well into the night. (See retreat schedule above for details.) It's this kind of variety and carefully planned activities that make retreats so successful. Small group activities are very specific and connected to that retreat's theme. For first-time participants, each new activity is an exciting adventure into themselves in a surprising and unique manner, and, since everyone is doing it (whatever "it" happens to be), no one needs to feel judgmental or above trying something new and different.

Sunday

Sunday is wrap-up day. Group members write warm fuzzies to one another, putting them into the bags that people have decorated and taped all around the walls of the community room. Group leaders give group members inexpensive gifts (such as lucky charm key chains or balls for group signatures) that they have carefully selected. During the last large group session in the spring, seniors have the opportunity to talk about how much CROYA has meant to them and to say goodbye on their last retreat. Students pack up, clean their rooms, and load the bus for home, tired and emotionally charged. Youth talk about their retreat weekend experiences below.

Fall versus Spring Retreat

The fall retreat is unique in that it remains essentially the same from year to year, with the same movie (kept top-secret by staff and youth) and the same themes. It is a prerequisite for all spring retreats, and one can attend the fall retreat only once, while eligible to attend the spring retreat every year. Exceptions are made for those students who come back for fall retreats in their junior and senior years to act as student retreat leaders. With the help of staff, youth retreat leaders do all the planning for the spring retreat, meeting in the subcommittee numerous times. Spring retreat is similar in structure and format, with variations on theme, icebreakers, games, and small group activities. (See Appendix for sample retreat forms.)

✆ Youth Comment on Retreat Experience

"I felt really comfortable talking about my problems with the group."

"I learned a lot about myself this weekend. And I noticed that other people noticed a lot of the good things about me. And the warm fuzzies that we did were really awesome and made people feel good, like when you were in the hot seat."

"Everyone really helped me get through some hard times. We talked about a lot of really hard stuff last night. Just having people there to comfort me helped a lot."

"I'm going back with a sense of knowing more about myself and others. And knowing that there are other people out there and you're not always alone. That's very important."

"I feel like I really got close with my group. I felt like I could say anything; I was totally comfortable. We had a lot of fun and we were also very serious at times too. As a retreat leader, I loved seeing the other side of it, because I remember when I was a member. Being a leader was a lot of fun. You guys should do it one year."

"Sometimes you feel like you're going through stuff that's bad, and it's good to see that everyone else goes through similar stuff and even though you might be completely different people, you still have the same emotions, thoughts and experiences."

"It was awesome."

"It rocked! It was great to get away, kick back and have fun."

CROYA's Most Excellent Adventure (Junior High)

CROYA's Most Excellent Adventure is the popular junior high version of a retreat. This one-day experience focuses on teamwork, trust, leadership, and responsibility. Using a format similar to the retreat's small group and large group activities throughout the day, this program also includes a four-hour outdoor experience at a nearby team challenge course. Teams of ten to twelve youth, led by a course facilitator and two high school students, move through a wooded area to work through physically and mentally challenging course activities.

Starting the day in typical CROYA fashion, young people meet at CROYA and are handed nametags by one of the high school student retreat leaders who will facilitate the day. On each nametag is written their name and beneath it a mysterious other name, such as Dawson, Homer, Monica, or Cindy. Starting out with a large group icebreaker, the group plays the donut game.

Donut Game

Youth form two large circles, one inner and one outer circle. People in the inner circle face out, while people in the outer circle face in, so people are looking at one another. When the music starts, the inner circle moves one way and the outer circle moves the other way. When the music stops, so do the people (as in musical chairs). A staff member then gives kids a question or a prompt to which they respond by talking to the person directly across from them—presumably someone they don't know at all or know very well. Some sample questions or prompts:

- **Where do you think you might want to go to college?**
- **If you could travel anywhere in the world, where would you go?**
- **Do you put mustard on any of your food; if so, which foods?**
- **What most excites you about Most Excellent Adventure?**
- **Tell a partner about the best dream you've ever had."**

Kids do five or six rounds to give everyone an opportunity to talk to a few people they don't know. Although some appear reluctant to talk to someone they may not know or like, this is a lively, successful icebreaker.

Small and Large Groups

The Donut Game is followed by introductions, the reading of rules, and a fun activity for having people find their small group members. A junior high student announces, "*Dawson's Creek* meets the *Brady Bunch*, *Friends* meet *The Simpsons*, and *ER* meets *Party of Five*," referring to the names of TV shows popular with kids. Youth then circulate giddily in a seemingly chaotic scene to find their groups and move into small group activities. Each person receives an Excellent Adventure packet, featuring a cover designed and decorated by young people, and containing everything they need for the day (including schedule, rules and goals, and activity sheets). This is a big event that has been planned by a youth subcommittee, who have met several times with the junior high youth worker to select activities and food and assemble packets.

Small groups are prearranged carefully by CROYA staff and student leaders. They intentionally separate friends, mix up students from different schools, even out the boy/girl ratio, and make sure each group includes seventh- and eighth-graders. Diversity is a goal here, and at the end of the day, students often point out that they were glad for the opportunity to interact with kids they otherwise wouldn't have spent time with.

Small groups do a series of activities for the next hour, breaking briefly to bring lunch back to their groups. (See Excellent Adventure Schedule in this chapter.) At 11:30 everyone loads onto a bus for the twenty-minute ride to the team challenge course, where themes of the day will unfold through experiences most youth have never encountered.

The Challenge Course

Once onsite, the challenge course staff facilitators go over general rules with kids in the cabin-like headquarters of the course. Teams then go out to a big field accompanied by their assigned facilitator and one CROYA adult staff member or chaperone for some small group introductory exercises and icebreakers. For instance, they toss around a Koosh Ball while playing a name game. They also practice a trust exercise where one person, with his or her back to a partner, leans back with the faith that their partner will catch them. It's an introduction to the theme of trust and offers an opportunity to process team thoughts verbally. This also sets the stage for what to expect throughout the afternoon. Small groups now move into a wooded area where the challenge courses await.

Prior to each challenge, the team facilitator explains objectives and rules and encourages groups to spend a few minutes planning and discussing strategy. After groups have successfully or unsuccessfully completed each challenge, the facilitator engages participants in a discussion about what they learned and observed during that exercise. Teamwork, trust, leadership, and cooperation are inevitable themes kids uncover, but in a serious hands-on manner. Examples of some of the challenge courses are "stump or river crossing," "cement tunnels," "boxes," and "the wall."

For the cement tunnels, young people are challenged with crawling through two tunnels built into a hill, each about twenty feet long. One is extremely narrow; the only way to get through it is to lie on their stomachs with arms stretched above their heads, then shimmy and scoot all the way through. The tunnels are dark and dirty, and seem even longer once inside. The challenge is to overcome fear and to cheer on teammates as they crawl through.

Another challenge is the stump or river crossing. Each armed with one small tree stump, the kids' goal is to cross an imaginary river, outlined by two lines drawn in the dirt. The river is filled with acid and there is a "no talking zone" and a swamp monster that can steal any stump left unattended for even a second. To make things more interesting, one or two members may be blindfolded as well. To accomplish the crossing, participants must rely on ingenuity, planning, teamwork, and trust.

After four hours of these challenges, youth take a bus ride back—hungry, dirty, and energized by their experience. They reassemble at CROYA for more large and small group activities, dinner, and a closing candle ceremony.

Experiences and Lessons Learned

The large group processes such questions as "What was the hardest situation for your group to tackle? How did you work together to accomplish this? Were you ever in a scary or uncomfortable position? Discuss one situation where someone from your group took on a leadership role."

Small groups go off to different rooms to participate in an activity that encourages them to talk about memories, dreams, fears, hobbies, and what makes them happy. All of their thoughts are inscribed on the various parts of what will become a nature collage—the trunk and leaves of a tree, a piece of the sun, flowers and bees. (See Appendix.) They also discuss questions, such as "What is the hardest thing in your life right now and how are you dealing with it?" or "Do you have any friends that you really worry about?" Kids respond by talking about things such as fighting with friends, deciding which college to go to, and friends who might have eating disorders.

Prior to the day, high school leaders have bought inexpensive symbolic gifts for their group members. At the end, everyone reconvenes for the closing candle ceremony and each participant is also given a small scented candle from CROYA. With the lights turned low and soothing music in the background, each person lights his or her candle from the person before them, then talks for a moment about what their Excellent Adventure experience has meant to them.

Excellent Adventure Schedule

10:00 A.M. Arrive at CROYA
   -Pick up name tags
   -Icebreaker (Donut Game and GOTCHA!)
   -Introductions—CROYA staff and chaperones, retreat leaders
   -Goals and Rules (read by high school retreat leaders)
   -Leaders get their groups together (TV show game—see above)
10:30–11:30 Small Group Activities—split up around CROYA facility
   -Small group icebreakers—choose two

1.Quote share

2. Hot seat!

3. Silently line up by birthdate

4. Picture/statement

-I AM

-Friendship worksheet (See Appendix)

-Individual goals—Discuss what students want to achieve today.

** Grab lunch and eat in groups

11:30   Bus to challenge course

12:00 – 4:00P.M. Challenge Course

4:45   Back at CROYA—Large Group Discussion

(Facilitated by high school retreat leaders)

5:15   Dinner Break

5:45   Small Group Work

(split up around CROYA facility)

Tree Collage Activity (See Appendix)

Small group discussion

(bag of questions / group feelings)

(See Appendix)

6:30   High Fives and Small Group gifts

Students write warm fuzzies on cut out paper hands ("high fives") to everyone in their group.

Group leaders give out small gifts such as play-dough, bubbles, sippy cups, jelly beans.

6:40   Large group reconvenes

Ending Activities

Large group gift (scented candles)

Candle Ceremony (See above)

Evaluations of Excellent Adventure

Evening Fun Time

The day's structured events end with youth invited to stay at CROYA to watch a movie, hang out, play games, etc. until 9:00 P.M. The downtime offers casual networking for staff and kids who haven't met before. Often, students from different schools who haven't come to other CROYA events come to Excellent Adventure, so it's an opportunity to connect and encourage them to keep coming. Kids talk about it for weeks afterward and encourage friends to go when it comes around each year.

ℂ℥ Youth Comment on Excellent Adventure Experience

"I learned that there are no limits. Nothing is impossible if you stay focused and aren't afraid to ask questions and ask for help. If you're willing, you can do anything."

"Teamwork is a big part of a lot of things, especially conquering your fears."

"Give other people a chance and you'll realize they're not that different."

"This was an eye opening experience. Without my team I couldn't have done things like the tunnel. It made me understand who I am."

"Even though you may not think you can, you really can trust others and rely on them."

Planning Retreats

CROYA has been conducting retreats for nearly fourteen years. The sample retreat and Excellent Adventure schedules and descriptions presented here are variable, and meant to give other communities an idea of the type of format and activities typical of CROYA retreats. They vary from retreat to retreat and have evolved with time and experience. As with everything involving youth, the possibilities are endless. CROYA is fortunate to have found a camp in Wisconsin that can accommodate up to ninety people for such weekends, and to have a team challenge course located in a neighboring community. The waiting lists referred to earlier are due simply to space limitations. As with all CROYA events requiring signup and limits, participation is on a first come, first served basis (except for student retreat leaders and chaperones, who are guaranteed a spot). Planning retreats is a labor-intensive process, both for staff and student planning committees, but their value is reinforced after each retreat by the youth, who are profoundly affected by their participation. (See Appendix for Retreat forms.)

9

Social Events

CRO

"Matt loved CROYA because the 'mothers' were not there."

— Susan Bryant, mother

WHILE CROYA'S PROGRAMMING is often educational, staff and student leaders spend a lot of time planning and executing events and activities that are really just for fun. While the original intention of the adults who conceived CROYA was to plan "activities to keep youth busy, structured and programmed," CROYA today strives to help young people feel ownership and commitment by having *them* do the actual planning and implementation of *their* chosen activities. They, not the CROYA staff, are the organizers and the doers.

Some of these events have become annual traditions, like "Battle of the Bands," while others, such as dances, occur periodically throughout the year. These are the kinds of events that require the youth subcommittees talked about in Chapter Six. Depending on what events are upcoming, committees will meet during lunches and after school (for the junior high) or during Wednesday Dinner Meeting (for the senior high), as often as is necessary to plan the event. Planning a concert takes several planning meetings, while planning a dance may require only one. The following events, categorized by type, i.e., "Concerts" or "Games" are CROYA's stockpile of good ones that work and that teens love. But each year they try some new ones, adding them if they work or moving on to others if they don't.

Concerts

Battle of the Bands

This annual event has the look of a bona fide rock concert, with sound checks all day long on the day of the "Battle," psychedelic lights and fog, and a professional sound crew with high-tech equipment. The Battle of the Bands, which is co-sponsored with Club Beat, a local non-profit organization funded by the Volunteer Bureau, was started in mid-1980s, and has grown in sophistication and popularity over the years. It is called "Battle of the Bands" because bands compete to be one of two bands chosen to have the first opportunity to play at CROYA's annual Lake Forest Day Band Jam in August and Summer Jam, at Lake Forest Beach in June.

The senior high youth worker, Todd, begins preparations months in advance of the concert, booking the auditorium and sound equipment, notifying interested bands of the date and pre-"Battle" meetings, and arranging for judges and chaperones. One criterion for entry is that a majority of the members in each band must be students at Lake Forest High, which includes residents of Lake Forest, Lake Bluff, and Knollwood, and only one member can have already graduated from high school. They must also register in advance, submitting an audition video of one song that they plan on performing in the show and attend an event-planning meeting at CROYA.

The style of music ranges from hard rock to alternative, '60s hippie to punk and more, with varying degrees of originality and talent. For the most recent Battle, *Smokin' Joe and the West Side Brass* was up first. They were impressive, with their lead guitarist on vocals and their brass section—complete with trumpets, saxophones and trombones.

The Battle of the Bands audience, made up of youth, range from stereotypical teens to serious "rockers," some with spiked and neon-dyed hair or body piercing. Parents of performers occasionally stop by throughout the evening to watch, and videotape their kids onstage.

The concert is long, starting at 7:30 P.M. and ending at about 11:30 P.M. Each band has a half-hour to play, and there are ten minutes between bands for equipment changes and setup.

During the concert, three judges score each band in the following categories, each worth 10 points for a total possible score for each band of 150 points:

- **Originality**
- **Showmanship**
- **Crowd response**

- **Musicianship**
- **Overall appearance**

Tickets are sold in advance for $5.00 apiece by band members, and at the door for $6.00. CROYA obtains non-removable wristbands for the night, issuing special color-coded wristbands for bands, crew, and volunteers. A professional program is printed, featuring band names, individual band members' names, and a performance schedule. It also gives credit to co-sponsors, including CROYA, Gorton Community Center (which donates the space), and a local music gallery and a recording studio, which provide prizes in the form of merchandise and recording time.

This event is relatively costly to put on and is not done for profit. Things like sound equipment are expensive, but CROYA generally breaks even with ticket revenues. Even when they don't, it's an important way in which to recognize youth who are committed to music to the extent that they have organized and practiced with a band that can perform at this level. It also serves to attract other young people to a CROYA event, both as participants and spectators. This is a good example of CROYA's diversity in programming to meet the needs and desires of a wide range of youth, and their efforts to create partnerships with other local organizations as often as they can.

Lake Forest Day Band Jam

During the annual Lake Forest Day carnival in August, CROYA is present in one quadrant of the tennis courts nearby, offering an alternative to rides and carnival games. Band Jam is a byproduct of Battle of the Bands, which takes place earlier in the year. The top two bands from "The Battle" win the honor of performing at Band Jam. Separated from the beer garden by a fence, kids congregate on the bleachers or in front of the stage to listen to their favorite local youth bands.

Many college students attend summer CROYA events like this one. Hugs and backslapping abound when CROYA alumni make the effort to stop by and say hello. And they are just as eager to catch up with CROYA staff as they are with old friends. This is yett another testament to the bonds that CROYA staff members have forged with students. They are truly happy to see former CROYA young adults and are interested in what is going on with them.

Summer Jam

Summer Jam is an annual concert held at the Lake Forest Beach. While this may conjure images of Woodstock, it is really a very low-key, well-executed event that youth, staff and other beach goers enjoy. The first Summer

Jam was held in 1982, after an unsuccessful effort in the prior year (See Chapter Two) and was very different from what it has evolved into today.

Often the same bands, made up of local youth, will play at CROYA's Battle of the Bands, Band Jam, and on their parade floats. (See Chapter Nine.) Setting up in the pavilion at the Lake Forest beach, four bands play for 30–45 minutes each. CROYA has reserved the pavilion and sound equipment and has arranged for adequate power supply as well. In addition, a local grocery store is onsite selling barbecued chicken and burgers, corn on the cob and watermelon. This year, a local game owner even offered to come and set up carnival games for free. Summer Jam is hosted by CROYA, which pays the cost of sound equipment, game prizes, food and tee shirts for student workers. Young people help in the food concession, sell CROYA tee shirts, and help videotape, among other jobs.

The senior high youth worker announces the bands on a microphone, and videotapes segments of the concert for airing on a future "CROYA Goes Cable" show. (See Chapter Seven.) Mostly junior high students, who tend to participate more in the summer activities CROYA offers, attend Summer Jam, but it is open to all youth, whether active in CROYA or not, as well as beach goers wanting to enjoy the concert and food. It's a fun, carefree summer event that is a tribute to CROYA's ability to accomplish seemingly complicated events with ease and enjoyment.

Dances

While dances are social in nature, CROYA's main goal in sponsoring them is, as always, to have youth plan and run the events.

Junior High Dances
Hollyball

This is the biggest annual dance for junior high students (grades 7 and 8). It takes place shortly after New Year's, during a month when kids need something to do. For many, it's their first semi-formal event and a reason to get dressed up. Girls put their hair up with fancy barrettes or sparkling tiaras, while boys typically wear shirts, ties and sport coats, only to remove their jackets once inside.

At 7:00 P.M. on the Friday night of the dance, over 650 kids descend upon the Lake Forest Intermediate School, having been dropped off out front. The seven-dollar tickets, designed by CROYA youth in subcommittee, have been sold in advance at school lunches. Coats fly as eager students make their way through the cafeteria, where tables, refreshments, and the professional photographer are set up, to the gym, which is darkened and decorated for Hollyball. The DJ has been armed with a list of song requests and song "no-no's," as well as fog and special lighting for the evening.

As the evening wears on, many couples dance, their arms resting on one another's shoulders and hips. An outsider looking in would be struck by the image of tall girls dancing with shorter boys, as is typical of this age group. It's also funny to observe a group of boys strategizing on the side. All at once they break up, heading for girls. A few are successful in their bids for dances; the others retreat back to the group to await the next song and burst of courage.

Prizes are awarded at Hollyball, too. Staff scopes out the action, thinking up spontaneous and random categories for prizes. They might run over and give a guy a prize for "the craziest tie" or give a whole group prizes just because they are "having fun." Prizes are usually gift certificates for the local pizzeria, bagel shop, Gap, or movie coupons. CROYA tee shirts are also given as prizes.

A particularly stressful part of the evening for CROYA staff and volunteer chaperones is pickup time, which is ten o'clock. All 650 kids are eagerly attempting to find their rides in a cold and crowded parking lot where parents are equally keen to pick up and get out. But CROYA staff handles this with their usual forethought and positive attitude. This year, the police agreed to be on hand to help out. And staff uses walkie-talkies to communicate from outside to inside. Those stationed outside will ask drivers the names of the youngster(s) they are picking up, then radio inside where CROYA staff calls out those names to kids huddled inside awaiting rides.

After eleven years, this is a much-anticipated event. As students leave, each is handed a picture frame on which reads "CROYA HOLLYBALL." In the weeks following the dance, Gretchen passes out Hollyball feedback forms at youth meetings and in schools for use in planning future Hollyballs and dances.

Other Dances

CROYA hosts two other junior high dances each year, in the fall and in the spring. While still well attended, these dances are simpler to put on. There are minimal decorations and food. Students pay at the door, which eliminates the need for advance ticket sales at schools. CROYA gives out prizes at these dances, such as CROYA tee shirts and gift certificates to local merchants like Sweets. Prizes are awarded for noncompetitive fun reasons, such as original dancing, wearing a crazy tie, having a great time, or any spontaneous reason a staff member thinks of.

High School Dances
Winter Formal

Girls in black dresses and high-heeled strap shoes run, coatless, through a slushy January night into the steamy cafeteria where this annual high school dance is in full swing. One of three annual dances co-sponsored by CROYA and the LFHS Student Council, the Winter Formal is another example of how far CROYA has come in its relationship with schools and its ability to host meaningful events for students. By 9:30 the cafeteria is packed and students are well into dancing and socializing.

Decorations are minimal and just what students asked for. A penguin ice sculpture adorns one corner, while strobe lights up on the senior stage give students and excuse to show off their dancing. In addition, there are some tables with balloons and streamers and a table with ice and soda. Since evening plans for the high school students usually include dinner, refreshments are kept simple. Tickets are sold in advance at lunchtime, and at the door. When students check in, their hands are stamped and they can vote for Snow Queen and Ice King, who have been nominated during ticket sales prior to the dance. About halfway through the dance, one of the teacher chaperones collects the ballots to be tallied.

Only in the last five years has the Winter Formal become a smooth-running and popular event among students. This is partially a result of Hollyball's success and the hard work done by CROYA and the Student Council. When an issue like underage drinking arises, CROYA is quick to make it an agenda item at weekly youth meetings. They process events that took place and brainstorm ways to avoid similar occurrences in the future.

Turnabout

Taking place in April right after spring break, this dance is a gender role reversal, with females asking males to be their dates.

Games

Jell-O Wrestling

"Something you do for three minutes, but remember the rest of your life."

— Lindsey Jeannides, CROYA youth

This activity falls under the category of good clean fun, despite the fact that it gets rather messy. The build-up for Jell-O wrestling is big, with youth planning costumes and strategy ahead of time, and volunteering to make clear Jell-O at home.

On the day of the event, staff and student helpers cover the rug area of CROYA with large tarps taped together and then taped to the floor. This is a big draw for CROYA, so the facility fills up early in anticipation of the seven o'clock start. Some CROYA alumni on spring break from college make time to stop by as well.

Interested youth have registered ahead of time with Todd, the senior high youth worker. Pairing up wrestlers for the three-minute matches, Todd takes into consideration gender, size, and the added lure of sibling rivalry. Students generally dress in shorts or workout clothes, and some paint slogans on their torsos for dramatic effect. One of the McPheeters chairs acts as referee. As the music and disco ball are turned on, the first bowls of Jell-O are tossed into the center of the tarp, and the first two wrestlers come out.

Each pair of wrestlers gets three one-minute rounds to impress the audience. It's hard to do much but roll around and laugh, since it is difficult to get hold of the opponent when Jell-O gets in the way. But that's the whole point. Try as one wrestler might to pin his or her opponent, just when they think they've got them, the other player slips from their hold.

Meanwhile, the crowd cheers and laughs at the Jell-O antics, while several people snap pictures to "capture the moment." Between one-minute rounds, friends act as coaches in the corners, giving the wrestlers pep talks and shoulder rubs. After each set, the audience votes for the winner with applause and cheers, but in the end everyone is pronounced a winner in this all-around good fun occasion. This event is a good example of CROYA's willingness and ability to push the limits. Four years ago, Jell-O wrestling was unheard of. Now it's become accepted and anticipated every year, and kids want to do even more. They are encouraged to think beyond what is normally acceptable and "shoot for the moon."

Photo Scavenger Hunt

When spring fever is high and students are eager for diversions from school and even CROYA meetings, the senior youth committee embarks on a photo scavenger hunt during a Wednesday youth meeting. CROYA staff borrows seven to ten instant cameras, buys film, and comes up with challenging and funny scavenger items. Groups of four to six youngsters load into cars and sport utility vehicles (with an adult driver per car) for an hour of goofiness, daring and healthy competition. Around town, kids can be seen clearly having a blast jumping in and out of cars as they run into local shops or make a pyramid in the Town Square. They meet back at CROYA after an hour or so to turn in their photos, determine the winner and receive prizes (usually in the form of gift certificates to local stores for ice cream, sweets, or bagels). Following are the rules and some scavenger item ideas that work for CROYA:

Guidelines
1. All drivers must be safety conscious. Do not compromise the safety of your group for that extra creative photo no matter how strongly your group pressures you, be smart!
2. You must arrive back at CROYA by 8:00 P.M. (Give youth a solid hour.)
3. Each camera is loaded with ten pictures.
4. You will be judged on your best eight pictures.
5. You may combine pictures to accumulate more points (example: a picture of the mayor and his dog is worth 100 + 50 points = 150 points).
6. Do not put yourselves or others in danger to obtain any of the pictures. Doing so will disqualify your group from the competition.
7. A bonus for creativity will be awarded by the McPheeters chairs.

CATEGORY 1 (25 Pts.)
- Build a pyramid in Market Square
- Spell CROYA with bodies
- All group members climb a tree

CATEGORY 2 (50 PTS.)
- Doing a good deed
- All group members in a bathroom stall
- All group members with a police officer
- Cross-dressing (25 pts. for each individual cross dresser)

CATEGORY 3 (75 PTS.)
- All wearing the same brand of shoes
- Standing on your heads in the Lake Bluff Gazebo
- Trying on clothes at a retail store

CATEGORY 4 (100 PTS.)
- At a sit down restaurant with people you don't know
- On a trampoline
- Two people in the group swimming (25 extra points for each additional group member swimming)

BONUSES (If you bring these things back you get 25 extra points)
- A feather
- Grey Poupon Mustard
- Tube socks
- Animal print underwear
- An orange toothbrush

Parades

CROYA participates in two annual parades, the Lake Bluff Fourth of July Parade and the Lake Forest Day Parade in August. Parade planning involves securing a flat bed and a truck (the Lake Forest Parks Department lends its vehicle for towing the float), and doing what is called "float building" with youth. For two weeks before the parade, CROYA staff meets youth out in the parking lot of CROYA for several hours' float building each day. This is almost as much fun as the parade itself, with music, refreshments, and an opportunity to flex their creative muscles.

The CROYA float on parade day is something to see, with "CROYA Loves Kids" on one side and "Happy Fourth of July" on the other, but that is not the most significant part. CROYA's float boasts a live rock band (again made up of local youth), playing very loud music throughout the parade. With a gasoline-powered generator in the back of the pickup truck and lots of CROYA youth hanging off the float, they are an example of American youth today—loud, carefree, and a bit defiant. The CROYA float is always at the end of the parade, just before the fire trucks and ambulances pull up the rear. With nearly 100 floats, that's pretty far back. This is perhaps because their music is so loud and can range from "headbanging" to rap to more traditional rock 'n' roll, but most likely it's because this is such a fun, youth-oriented way to end the parade with a bang. CROYA youth and staff don't mind, viewing it almost as an honor to be at the end. People have noticed them enough to think about where they should be placed. Youth have made their mark and they're proud of it.

The CROYA float is one of the best examples of CROYA's philosophy— that it be youth-driven. When challenged with what kind of float to have, CROYA youth wanted a rock band on board—a band that could play whatever they wanted as loud as they wanted. One might envision crowds of people looking on in distaste because of the music, but what happens is quite the opposite. While not everyone enjoys loud rock music, people of all ages wave, cheer, smile, and dance in the streets to CROYA's float. It is 100 percent kids and that's why it works. People see that and applaud the fact that kids are doing this rather than less constructive things. When CROYA's float passed the viewing stand at the most recent Fourth of July Parade, the band gave it their all with a Jimi Hendrix rendition of "The Star-Spangled Banner." And for the past five years, CROYA's float has placed first or second. What better way to celebrate our nation's birth and our youth?

Other Fun Stuff

Days Off

On days when schools are closed, such as Martin Luther King Jr. Day or holiday breaks, CROYA organizes casual fun activities for whoever wants or needs something to do. They often rent a movie and buy pizza to bring to the CROYA facility, or try something different, like ice skating in the local park. Studies have shown that offering young people opportunities for diversion during otherwise unoccupied time is a way to keep them engaged in positive, healthy activities and discourage loitering and what may lead to negative pursuits.

Outings

Outings are field trips of sorts, mostly for junior high students. Youth planning committees decide where to go and help with planning tasks. Here are a few CROYA favorites:

Baseball Game—Every year, CROYA takes a busload of kids to a Cubs game in Chicago. They usually go on 70s Night, dressed up in retro attire to get into the spirit and possibly on TV.

Taste of Chicago—CROYA takes a busload of kids to this annual event in downtown Chicago, where kids and staff sample a variety of foods, watch performances and fashion shows, and enjoy amusement park rides.

Bowling—Once or twice during the school year, CROYA youth go bowling—sometimes "COSMIC Bowling—at local lanes. This trip usually includes dinner at a pizzeria.

Skate on State—Junior high youth initiated this program this year, including ice skating at Skate on State in downtown Chicago, and dinner at Ed Debevics, a Chicago-based restaurant chain.

Post-CROYA Activities

Kids often extend their informal social time together after a CROYA meeting or event. Sometimes they hang out as late as a staff member will stay at the facility. Other casual activities include excursions to local eateries like the Full Moon Diner, video game rooms, or someone's house to watch TV or listen to music. This year, inspired by a community "polar bear plunge" fundraiser as well as by post-retreat enthusiasm, young people headed down to the local beach to plunge into Lake Michigan after a youth meeting in March. This proved to be very exciting, which only inspired them to "do it again!" week after week. Encouraging anyone interested in joining them, the group grew each week and turned into a bonding experience for those involved. They'd immediately come back to CROYA, shivering and bragging about their plunges to anyone who would listen.

Road Trips

Planned by the executive committee vice chair, road trips are simply high school excursions to youth-chosen locations. These trips tend to be hard to organize, with teens busy with school activities and sometimes reluctant to participate in group outings on weekends. The one road trip that has become an annual ritual is the haunted house at the Museum of Science and Industry, in Chicago. This comes with all the field trip necessities: permission slips, separate fee, and a bus.

Tee Shirts

> *"CROYA tee shirts are popular at school, and they help spread the CROYA spirit!"*
>
> — Jenny Sarkela, CROYA executive committee

Every year, CROYA youth design both the junior and senior high CROYA tee shirts. These are the shirts that will be given out for community service project work, prizes and awards throughout the year at CROYA. While students can purchase one, they are encouraged to do a CSP. In the fall, announcements are made for interested students wishing to submit art designs for the tee shirts. After the submission deadline, staff displays the artwork at CROYA and asks youth to vote on their designs of choice at a weekly meeting. Students vote for two designs per tee shirt, for the front and back of each. Staff also solicits youth input in terms of tee shirt colors, sleeve length, and sizes. The artists then meet with CROYA staff, giving their ideas on colors for the actual designs. Staff then meets with the tee shirt company to work out the details, and then generally orders about 300 shirts.

⌘ Youth Comment on Social Events

"Where else can you Jell-o wrestle?"

"CROYA is a place where those of us in bands get opportunities to play."

"CROYA does a lot more fun activities at the school than anyone else. They make the dances more fun, because anyone can come."

10

Icebreakers and Games

⟨ॐ⟩

Icebreakers

ICEBREAKERS ARE SELF-EXPLANATORY in definition only. Coming up with creative ways for people to start meetings and loosen up is another challenge CROYA staff and students face. Over the years, though, they've amassed a collection of quick, effective icebreakers that lend themselves to interpretation and variation. Most involve going around the circle and giving everyone a chance to respond. A sampling of creative icebreakers follows.

Quick Icebreakers

Chat-a-Chini ® Learned Enterprises International, Lake Mills, WI 1994— leader passes around bag full of little slips of paper with a question on each. Participants take turns answering one of the questions.

Examples:

• If you could live someone else's life for a week, would you want to, and if so, whose would you pick?

• What is it most difficult for you to say "no" to?

• If you could be the most attractive, the most athletic, or the smartest person in your class, which would you pick and why?

• If you were given $5 million to spend helping other people, how would you spend it?

• What are your favorite ways to renew your energy?

• What is your favorite candy bar and/or what is your favorite color and why?

• Share with us your ultimate meal, if you could have any food you wanted. (This is a fun one, with kids' responses ranging from "a super Italian meal by my grandma" to "Chinese food with a lot of chocolate, but not together!")

Longer, Activity-Type Icebreakers

× Bring in bags of M&M candy. Give each participant a handful, which they separate by color. Each color becomes a category, such as "What is your goal in life?" "Share a childhood memory." "Who is your hero, who do you look up to and why?"

× Have a larger group go on a human scavenger hunt to get to know people. Give them a list of things to find out: "Find someone with the same color eyes as you." "Find someone who plays the violin (or baseball, etc.)." "Find someone who has a birthday in the same month as yours." "Find someone who has traveled to another country."

× Bring a roll or two of toilet paper. Have each person tear a length. Depending on how many sheets they've gotten, each person tells that many things about themselves to the group or to a partner.

Seasonal Icebreakers

× What is your favorite Halloween movie? Students are surprisingly open about discussing their fears for this one. One student described watching a movie at his friend's house one night. As he walked home, he was startled by raccoons, and was very aware of the dark and shadows. He unabashedly told everyone he ran home in a "full-out sprint."

× What was your most memorable holiday gift?

× What are you doing for the upcoming holiday/break?

× What was your favorite thing about spring break?

Retreat Icebreakers

× Using an adjective that starts with the same letter as your name, describe yourself. Kids say things such as "Jumpy Jill," "Radical Ryan," "Cheeky Claire," and "Amazin' Aashish."

(See Chapter Eight for detailed descriptions of more retreat icebreakers.)

Peer Training Icebreakers
(taken from the Peer Training Manual)

All peer-training sessions follow the same format. Students and the facilitator sit on the floor in a circle. During the icebreaker, one person begins, then that person chooses another to go next.

× For first session, each person shares his or her
  - name
  - year in school

- Something he/she looks forward to or something good that has recently happened.
- Share something good that happened to you this week.
- What is/are your goal(s) for yourself this year?
- If you were an animal, what kind would you want to be?
- How has the school year been going for you so far this year?
- If you could change something about the world, what would you change?
- In terms of emotions, ways of thinking, and behavior with friends, what are some of the differences between males and females?
- Name three things you like most about your best friend(s).
- How do you think your peer training group has been? Do you think the group participated willingly and was really interested? How well do you think you have learned the material? What was the strength of your group? Its weakness?

Ask one of the participants to think of an icebreaker and start it.

Talk about the differences between men and women and how they interact. (This tied in with a peer-training session on "responding skills" and understanding how to relate to different people.)

✂ Youth Comment on Icebreakers

"I like icebreakers because half the time you don't know people. It helps you start talking."

"Icebreakers also help the leaders."

"A lot of CROYA is about the comfort level. With icebreakers and games, you can't be embarrassed."

"It's a lot harder to betray someone's trust once you've gotten to know them."

Games

CROYA is kids, and kids, no matter how old they get, love to play games. CROYA uses games at the end of every youth meeting, during retreats, and at other appropriate meetings and programs to allow youth to have fun and release energy. The staff can't help but join in and have fun too. Some games are played regularly; others are annual events. February is "Love Month" at CROYA, with various love games, such as

"Singled Out" and "The Dating Game" (modeled after the popular televisions shows of the same names), featured throughout the month. These often dominate the weekly youth meetings, with the business portion kept to a minimum. The McPheeters (games) chairs are in charge of thinking up and running the games. At other events, such as retreats, student retreat leaders and staff agree upon games. CROYA relies upon youth ideas, past experience, books, and other resources to find ideas for games. Here are a few of the favorites of CROYA youth. (See Chapter Eight for more retreat game ideas.)

Singled Out

CROYA recreates the popular teen dating game, based on the MTV show "Singled Out." It gives four single kids a chance to find a significant other. To give everybody a chance to win, they play two rounds. A host asks questions and facilitates the game. First, one guy sits behind a screen and asks a series of questions to narrow down the "dating pool of girls." Everyone has already filled out questionnaires, so the questions are answered quickly. A sample question: "Do you like girls with makeup or natural?" The guy answers, and all the girls who didn't pick that answer are required to leave the "pool." They are eliminated one by one, until three finalists remain. Then, the final big question is answered and that winner gets tickets to a dance sponsored by CROYA. Then the girls and guys switch places and it all happens again.

Ultimate Frisbee

This is similar to football, but is played with a Frisbee and slightly different rules. Divide into two teams, an even number of people on each. One team throws the Frisbee ("kickoff"). The receiving team gets it, passing to other team members without moving more than five steps each. The objective is to advance the ball and get a touchdown. If a team member fumbles the Frisbee, play automatically switches to the other team at the spot where the Frisbee landed.

Photo Scavenger Hunt

Kids go around the community taking instant camera pictures of their team members doing things or getting things on a list. The first team back to CROYA with eight qualifying pictures wins. (See Chapter Nine.)

Karaoke

CROYA rents a Karaoke Machine and the kids sing along. Often, the CROYA cable crew will videotape the fun. (See Chapter Seven, "CROYA Goes Cable.")

Kickball

Like baseball, only using kickball, this oldie is still good fun for youth.

Capture the Flag

The object is to find a hidden flag and run it back to your team's side without getting tagged. Each team has a flag (e.g., a towel) to hide. Once the team crosses the mid-line to the opposite side, they're eligible to get tagged, then sit in the other team's "jail." Once you're in jail, the only way to get out is if someone from your own team tags you out. Then that person is eligible for a free walk back. CROYA youth usually play a couple of rounds.

Pictionary

Like the popular game named "Pictionary," two teams try to guess the same subject simultaneously, with each group in front of a dry-erase easel. The first team to get it wins. Repeat for multiple rounds.

Donut Bowl (or Cup)

CROYA youth play football or hockey with the local police as a way of keeping the lines of communication open. Families are invited and food is served. This takes a lot of coordination to get scheduled, but it's worth it.

Dating Game

Mimics the popular TV game show, creating props as needed to simulate the set.

Price is Right

Based on the popular TV game show, three contestants guess the prices of such things as toothpaste, razors, pens, and other low-priced items. CROYA youth make a cardboard wheel. The person who guesses the item priced the most over a dollar gets to stay for the final round. Winners receive prizes of silly toys, like bubbles, pizza, and gift certificates to local merchants.

Balloon Stomp

Distribute one balloon and a three-foot length of ribbon to each person. Have them blow up the balloon, tie the ribbon around the balloon, then around their ankle. The object of the game is to be the last person with an intact balloon. Using music to periodically begin and stop the "stomping," players attempt to break other players' balloons. People whose balloons are broken must step out. The last player with a balloon wins a small prize.

Additional Resources

CROYA staff continually accesses resources for additional game and icebreaker ideas. Here's a list of some books they have found helpful:

Apacki, Carol. *Energize!* Newark, Ohio: Quest International, 1991. ISBN# 1-56095-059-5

Jackson, Tom. *Activities That Teach.* Cedar City, Utah: Red Rock Pub., 1993, 1994, 1995. ISBN # 0-916095-49-5

Jackson, Tom. *More Activities That Teach.* Cedar City, Utah: Red Rock Publishing, 1995. ISBN # 0-916095-75-4

Rice, Wayne and Yaconelli, Mike. *Play It!: Over 400 Great Games for Groups.* Grand Rapids, Michigan: Zondervan Publishing House, 1986. ISBN # 0-310-35191-X

West, Edie. *201 Icebreakers: Group Mixers, Warm-ups, Energizers, and Playful Activities.* New York: McGraw Hill, 1997. ISBN # 0-07-069600-4 (PBK) and ISBN # 0-07-069599-7 (LL)

CB Youth Comment on Games

"After the more serious meeting, we want to have some fun."

"The games are run by students. It makes it more fun."

11

Building and Maintaining a Base of Support within the Community

CRADA

"CROYA has put credence in the things we do, because they are so respected in the community." ·

> — *Diane Tiffany, Volunteer Bureau*
> *of Lake Forest and Lake Bluff*

TODAY, CROYA'S PLACE in the community is strong. It is looked upon as an advocate and expert on youth, providing a vital community service. And while problems with youth have not disappeared over CROYA's twenty-year existence, the community has not experienced the teen suicides and teen violence that precipitated the organization's birth two decades ago. CROYA answers a need for a large number of young people and does so with the support of city officials, schools, parents and other community members.

But this wasn't always the case. In the beginning, CROYA had to prove itself in order to survive and maintain funding. Over time, CROYA staff worked hard to break down barriers and establish strong working relationships with the schools. They earned the trust of youth, despite obstacles and setbacks along the way, and they established strong ties with other community organizations, with which they now work closely. All of this is just as important to maintaining and growing a youth agency as the actual work they do with young people.

Resources and Partnerships

Financial Commitment

Obtaining some initial financial commitment from the community, whether from local government or an organization such as the United Way, is essential. People don't necessarily have buy-in at first, so it is important to hire at least one paid employee—even if part-time to start—who is responsible for developing relationships with the community's youth, educating adults on the "process" and acting as a conduit between the two groups.

Influential Adult Board

Establishing a strong adult board, made up of influential people in the community, is critical. The board does a lot of the work in the early days, including hands-on work with youth, but the payoff is enormous. A lot of credibility is gained by virtue of the fact that powerful community members and leaders are backing the youth agency. It puts the necessary political peer pressure on people who are empowered to make, or not make, things happen. Board members can help open reluctant doors to give the youth a chance to prove themselves.

A good example of this is the first Summer Jam that CROYA held in 1982. Youth had worked hard on committees for months developing proposals, anticipating problems, and planning every last detail of a concert that many adults saw as controversial. When it came down to securing a location, many turned the young people down, clearly unwilling to take what they saw as a big risk.

It was then that the president of Lake Forest College, Eugene Hotchkiss, stepped up and agreed to let CROYA hold its concert on the grounds of the college. A member of the CROYA board and instrumental in the organization's birth, Dr. Hotchkiss capitalized an opportunity to do something other adults were reluctant to do—have faith in the ability of young people to plan and implement programs they wanted while taking responsibility for the outcome. At the same time, he was sending an important message to everyone in the community. By putting his reputation and the college's facilities on the line, he was setting a high standard for community investment and involvement in the needs of youth, and perhaps daring anyone to question CROYA's validity.

The concert was a success despite having been forced indoors to the college's field house by inclement weather. And it turned out to be a huge public relations success for CROYA.

Strong Ties with Schools

The third key element in establishing support within the community is developing strong ties with schools. Young people spend a large portion of their time at school, so it is critical that staff has access to schools and good working relationships with faculty, counselors, deans, principals, vice principals and other administrators. But in the early days, CROYA was relatively unknown and had not gained credibility with many people, including school officials. There was some hesitancy to have a group like CROYA inside the schools. Some school personnel were unsure of CROYA's purpose or role, and worried that CROYA would come in and tell them that what they were doing was wrong.

An important stride toward establishing a working relationship between CROYA and the schools occurred when Dr. Robert Metcalf, superintendent of the high school in CROYA's early years, embraced the organization's work. He was appointed to the CROYA board, which enabled him to affect change from both sides. His involvement enabled him to gain first-hand knowledge and appreciation of the work CROYA was doing, and thus act as a critical professional vehicle in administrative circles to break down any barriers that existed.

For example, Dr. Metcalf put the first youth chair on the All School Council, an embellishment of the Administrative Council. He also went to bat for CROYA on many occasions, helping secure additional funding from the schools so that CROYA staff could get away from administrative duties and spend more time in the schools with youth. He gave CROYA the use of a room adjacent to the cafeteria so they would have a place to meet, conduct peer training, and have a greater presence.

In time, CROYA and the high school made the transition from acting as two independent entities to working cohesively as one. Dr. Metcalf is credited with opening the doors of the schools to CROYA, and today CROYA is firmly entrenched in the culture and daily activities of the public schools. Former CROYA director Margot Martino comments, "CROYA gained more acceptance than we would have gotten if Bob Metcalf hadn't been there. The result is that CROYA is a valued part of the schools. Bob has a genuine love of the kids. Sometimes he and I would stand in the entrance of the school together identifying the names of the kids who walked through the doors. There were very few whom Bob didn't know."

CROYA's involvement with schools includes:

- CROYA staff is present in the schools on a dally basis, whether to teach peer training, touch base with youth working on upcoming programs and events, talk with faculty and administration, or simply connect with young people in the cafeteria. Their presence and familiarity are key to establishing their place within the youth world, both in and out of school. This also enables staff to know what's going on with kids in order to reach out to those in need, lend a friendly ear, and possibly circumvent problems.

- CROYA is linked to the student council, with an executive member of the student council also holding the position of student council liaison on CROYA's executive committee. This enables them to share information, have a voice in upcoming school activities (often co-sponsoring events), and work closely with faculty and non-CROYA youth.

- CROYA co-organizes and co-conducts peer training, with Lake Forest High School faculty, for about 125 youth per year. High school faculty is involved, often teaching some of the classes. CROYA uses high school classrooms and conducts Student-to-Student meetings and field service signups in the cafeteria and library. (See Chapter Seven.)

- CROYA sponsors and co-sponsors leadership training, both in the schools and in the CROYA facility. (See Chapter Seven.)

- CROYA works closely with faculty from various departments, including student assistance, special needs, and outdoor education. Developing relationships among different groups provides the opportunity to network, reaching different capacities of youth with diverse interests.

- CROYA develops relationships with custodial staff, who are invaluable when, for example, staff needs doors unlocked or tables and chairs for events.

- CROYA works closely with the secretaries and administrative staffs, sharing resources such as labels and mailing lists.

- School representatives such as the high school principal sit on the CROYA adult board.

- CROYA is considered a club within the high school, and well represented in the yearbook each year, with pictures of CROYA staff interacting with youth.

Working with Community-Based Organizations

"We have been inspired and schooled by CROYA in the finer points of working with teens."

— Diane Tiffany, Volunteer Bureau
of Lake Forest and Lake Bluff

Often, when people want to address youth needs, they come to CROYA for help. By virtue of its relationships with youth, CROYA can help pull kids into efforts in progress that staff thinks are worthwhile. For instance, when the Volunteer Bureau of Lake Forest and Lake Bluff wanted to establish a place for kids to hang out, they rallied CROYA's support and involvement in the process. The senior high youth worker sat on the "grotto group" committee and helped establish a youth board modeled on CROYA's. It was significant that it wasn't only CROYA youth on The Beanery (a coffee house), youth board. CROYA helped encourage youth attendance from a cross-section of young people, including all classes, genders and groups/cliques, not just CROYA kids. The CROYA Process was transferable and could work with any group of kids given the empowerment to make what they wanted happen.

Some of the community-wide meetings held to solicit input for The Beanery were even held at CROYA, demonstrating its support. CROYA was also an official supporter of The Beanery, with its name appearing on the brochure and signs. Once The Beanery was established, CROYA continued to network with youth in schools, talking it up and bringing in student bands to play. And the Volunteer Bureau board continues to solicit CROYA staff input as The Beanery evolves, bringing Club Beat to the forefront to suit the changing tastes and needs of youth.

In short, the community now sees CROYA as accessible to help with anything and everything connected with youth. CROYA advertises for worthwhile programs and events at weekly youth meetings, uses youth as an invaluable sounding board for ideas, and is eager to get involved if the staff thinks it is worthwhile for the community's young people.

As current director Kamy Daddono points out, "Youth are an emotional topic. There are always concerns and tragedies to deal with. When something needs to be done for youth, people rally; it's an easy arena in which to pull people together." For this community, they look to CROYA to help with that process, and CROYA is always ready and willing. They have sincerely and rightfully earned that reputation, which is another way they are entrenched within the community.

Community Ties and Exposure

Handling Mistakes Appropriately

Another unlikely way that CROYA engenders support is via its mishaps. When CROYA youth make a mistake, like scratching a car during a car wash or breaking a window during a retreat weekend, CROYA staff and youth are quick to step up and be accountable. When these rare events occur, CROYA uses such incidents to encourage dialogue among youth, holding meetings to "process" what happened and asking *youth* to recommend and decide what should be done. Young people decided to use half the proceeds from the car wash to pay for the scratch, for example, and logged community service hours to repay CROYA for replacing the window. And, of course, staff and youth offer sincere apologies to anyone negatively affected by their behavior. Even people quick to criticize CROYA find it hard to stay angry for long, with youth providing a refreshing example of responsible and caring young adults. These potential negatives are turned into positives by the way CROYA handles such situations.

Community Service

CROYA actively involves youth in community service projects in its own and neighboring communities throughout the year. (See Chapter Seven.) This yearly or regular contact between youth and organizations is a natural way to develop goodwill and support for CROYA's efforts.

Teenage Placement Service (TAPS)

Available since the early days of CROYA, this job posting service pro vides an invaluable aid to residents needing student workers and to students needing jobs. It is a way to help and to maintain contact with community members throughout the year. (See Chapter Seven.)

Community-Wide Meetings

CROYA is regularly asked to bring young people to community-wide meetings soliciting input on a range of issues, from hiring the new police chief to embarking on Partners for Progress, a healthier communities campaign. This wasn't always the case. In the early days, CROYA's director would represent youth at community meetings, knowing where they stood on issues and acting as their "voice."

The first time CROYA youth actively participated in decision making at a higher level than their own youth committee was in building the CROYA facility, erected in 1987. Youth helped in all phases of the project, from design and layout to furniture pricing and selection. They met often with the city manager, who found their analysis thorough and thoughtful. He came to respect their input, and they learned to listen to his feedback as well.

Where, in the past, CROYA often had to ask that youth be included, community leaders now think of CROYA youth as those who should be included in any community dialogue. (See Chapter One.)

The City of Lake Forest's Executive Team

As a member of the City of Lake Forest's executive team, the CROYA director networks with other city leaders, exerting CROYA's influence in subtle as well as obvious ways. She is abreast of what is happening at the higher level of city government, in a position able to give input and solicit support when needed. More importantly, she is seen as an important figure within the community—a respect that transfers to CROYA.

Experts on Youth

CROYA has rightfully come to be looked upon as the community's expert on youth. In addition to the ongoing important work they do with youth, CROYA staff stay abreast of regional and national youth issues and trends. They are constantly accessing current research materials on youth, attending pertinent seminars and training, and communicating within their own professional networks to keep current and informed on issues affecting young people. Perhaps most importantly, the staff of CROYA is genuine, with a sincere interest in youth. Current director Kamy Daddono says with pride, "Our only agenda is to enrich the lives of youth."

12

The Sensitive Issue of Counseling

"A cry for help can come in many different ways."

— Todd Nahigian, senior high youth worker

CROYA's ROLE IN COUNSELING, touched on briefly in other chapters, has been an issue that CROYA staff has grappled with over the years. What role in the "counseling" effort should staff play? What are their qualifications? What is their exposure? When is it appropriate for CROYA staff to informally counsel kids in need versus bringing in additional help? Should they hire a certified counselor on staff? The issue has been revisited from time to time in response to changing conditions and needs of youth. CROYA is comfortable with its role today, and the system they've established works.

Identifying Youth at Risk

One of the basic responsibilities of CROYA staff is early assessment of youth at risk. This identification process involves gauging the seriousness of the problem and determining the best means of helping the youth involved. As objective adults whom young people trust, they are in an ideal position to talk with individuals about their problems and determine if the seriousness of the situation warrants further involvement of school counselors, parents, and/or professionals. CROYA staff is continually talking among themselves about different students, what's going on with whom, and how to handle each situation. Always on hand to talk to a young person, CROYA staff are often the first adults to whom youth or friends of youth in trouble come for an ear to listen or for advice. CROYA staff has earned this trust and is careful with it, making thoughtful decisions on a case-by-case basis. And while CROYA has one trained counselor on staff, they do not act in that capacity when it comes to youth with serious problems. When a situation warrants involving parents and/or outside professionals, CROYA facilitates that process, acting as bridge for youth to the needed support services—school counselors, outside counselors or agencies, and/or parents.

And while this method has worked well for CROYA, determining when to help and when to seek help is not easily defined. The staff has become skilled in making these decisions through years of working together, interacting and building relationships with youth, and developing skills through additional training. Their case-by-case decisions take into consideration everything they know about the youth involved, the parents, and the available resources for additional help. There are no absolutes with issues having a range of seriousness. CROYA staff assess each situation and youth involved independently to take action that is in their best interest.

Some situations in which CROYA staff are comfortable working with youth informally:

- **Relationship problems—with parents, friends, girlfriends or boyfriends.**
- **Mild depression—indicated by a lack of a social network and activities or low self-esteem, for example.**
- **School-related problems—such as homework overload, issues with teachers or other students, stress about sports, etc.**
- **Eating disorders—at a very early stage.**
- **Alcohol and drug abuse—not addiction.**
- **Risky sexual behavior.**

Some areas in which CROYA staff refer out to additional help:

- **Suicidal ideation—exhibiting signs of seriousness as indicated by having and talking about a plan, having a means (such as a weapon), or demonstrating hopelessness.**
- **Chronic depression—as indicated by youth always being neutral or down but never in a good mood. Or, a youth comes and goes rather than participating consistently in CROYA. Speech may be consistently negative; the young person doesn't acknowledge any positives in life. Energy levels are low. Physical appearance and hygiene are poor.**
- **Manic depressive (Bipolar) disorder—indicated by being very "up" at times, very low at others.**
- **Advanced eating disorder—indicated by sudden weight loss or gain, and especially by friends talking about it.**
- **Drug and/or alcohol addiction—indicated by significant withdrawal from**

activities, school and friends, showing up to programs and events intoxicated, hiding and denying usage, depression, and consistently poor or unusual life decisions.

- Advanced antisocial behavior—indicated by youth breaking the law, not getting caught and bragging about it, or getting arrested.

Referral Process

If young people reveal to staff that they might have a condition that warrants further involvement, such as their safety being in jeopardy, the process of getting help varies. Normally, CROYA staff will call upon the school's counseling staff for assistance. This is always with the full knowledge and consent of the young person involved—sometimes it takes weeks of talking to them to get their consent. CROYA staff is careful not to betray the trust through which they have learned this information. They also encourage youth to discuss serious situations with their parents, but CROYA staff does not call parents and betray confidences unless the young people seem to be in danger of harming themselves.

In addition, depending on the age of the youth, it may or may not be mandated that the parents be notified. Part of CROYA's objective in its counseling effort with youth is for the youth to decide on their own whether to talk to parents and/or counselors. But the reality is that sometimes the parents are the source of the problem. This is where CROYA staff acts in a surrogate role, being trustworthy adults that kids can talk to. School counselors will take the next steps, sometimes counseling youth in school, or perhaps involving parents or recommending private counseling.

If a youth reveals a serious situation in which his or her safety is in jeopardy, however, it is incumbent upon CROYA staff to get that young person help immediately. At times this means that they will not leave the youth's presence until someone—a parent or counselor—has been brought in. While this is an extreme and rare example, it is important to mention. CROYA staff knows when the seriousness of a situation warrants immediate action, with or without student consent. Whenever young people seem to be in jeopardy of harming themselves or others, CROYA staff is quick to act.

When a "Friend" is in Trouble: CROYA's Role

Another scenario that often presents itself is one youth revealing concern about a friend to CROYA staff. This is a delicate situation, because while the young person may want to get help for the friend, they also want to protect that friend and preserve their own anonymity. When this situation arises, CROYA staff never asks the name of the friend in question; they wait until the youth is ready to reveal it, or they surmise who the friend might be. Because of their close relationships with a large number of youth, their presence in schools and in the youth world, CROYA staff is perceptive about what's going on, who's doing well and who might be in trouble.

Once staff thinks they know who the person is, they seek opportunities to talk informally with the youth. The opportunity might present itself at a weekly youth meeting or other CROYA event, or at school. Sometimes, if the youth has withdrawn from activities and CROYA, staff might phone them and say, "Hey, we haven't seen you around lately. How have you been? What's up? Do you want to have lunch?" They wait for the young person to offer an opening to discuss the issue in question, which youth often do. Kids are often eager to talk about their problems with a caring adult who doesn't judge, overreact, or threaten. Because of the relationships and trust they've developed with kids, CROYA staff are often the only adults with whom kids will take that risk. Staff is often able to help these "friends of friends" without ever betraying sources.

In summary, CROYA's role in the counseling effort is relational, not therapeutic. Staff acts as informal counselors for common teen problems, and as referral sources for more serious issues. They are in a prime position to do so, having earned the trust and confidence of so many young people. Through their ongoing relationship building with youth and their firm presence in the youth world, CROYA staff "has the pulse on the kids of this community," according to director Kamy Daddono, including a keen sense of how to help those in need.

☏ Youth Comment on Counseling

"I feel more comfortable going to someone at CROYA."

"CROYA staff have good listening skills. You see them once a week during free time, so there's an opportunity to talk if you need to."

"I sometimes just want a different perspective and the CROYA staff is always willing to listen."

"They don't judge you on what you say."

"CROYA is like a parent that doesn't ground you for making a stupid choice."

"CROYA staff helped me gain the confidence to talk to my parents about something that was bothering me."

"The staff always check in with me."

"When we come to the staff, it's not necessarily with a problem. But you always know you can go to them when you do have a problem."

13

Getting the Word Out

❧❧❧

THE SUCCESS OF CROYA'S MISSION depends on attracting as many youth as are interested to its meetings and programs. Over the years, they've developed an extensive database of youth, community leaders, and alumni, and have found various inroads and vehicles within the schools and the community for promoting CROYA. The best "sellers" are the young people who are involved and "talk it up" among friends and at school. But CROYA has found many other opportunities to get its name out so that kids identify CROYA with youth programming and fun and want to join in. This wasn't always the case. In early days, CROYA often had trouble getting recognition for its efforts. The organization would help with a community event, for instance, but no mention of its involvement would be made. That's not a problem today. CROYA's name is connected with "youth" and fun activities more often than not. CROYA sponsors and co-sponsors many events, happy to share the credit when other community organizations, such as the Volunteer Bureau, play a role. Here are some ways in which CROYA "gets the word out" to kids.

Communications

Monthly CROYA Calendar
Perhaps its best link to youth, CROYA sends out two calendars every month to every person on the mailing list, including approximately 750 to the junior high youth committee and 1200 to the senior high youth committee, in addition to teachers, counselors, the CROYA Adult Board, and city staff. Calendars are also posted on school bulletin boards. Like

everything else at CROYA, these calendars are fun and kid-friendly, with lots of pictures from recent CROYA events and nifty graphics to boot. Calendars list all meetings, events, activities, outings, deadlines, etc. These include all CROYA events, of course, and also significant happenings at the schools, like graduation, school breaks, proms, talent shows, etc. The flaps of these calendars (which are simple 8 x 11" colored copy paper, tri-folded and sent via bulk mail), are used for bigger, bolder reminders of important upcoming events, like the annual CROYA group picture or poinsettia fundraiser.

CROYA's mailing list is compiled manually by the staff. At every meeting or program they host, a mailing list sheet is sent around so students interested in receiving mailings can sign up voluntarily. In addition, at the end and beginning of each school year, CROYA solicits incoming seventh-graders during presentations, and gets as many of them on the mailing list as possible. At new student lunches throughout the year, CROYA asks interested students to sign up. Parents also call, and people stop by looking for information, and the staff always offers the opportunity to be on CROYA's mailing list. Being on the mailing list is purely voluntary and entails no obligation.

Flyers

For special events, upcoming meetings, or subgroup gatherings, CROYA regularly sends out flyers to targeted groups on the mailing list. These might be for an upcoming executive committee dinner meeting, an STS meeting or field experience, a large fundraiser or any other program that warrants individual reminders. CROYA has the process down to a science, with a database that segregates mailing labels, a megacopier, and a machine that folds flyers. Their bulk mailing permit keeps costs as low as possible.

Posters and Signs

Weekly, CROYA advertises throughout schools with posters made by youth and staff. For the senior youth committee, a poster board chair is responsible for making, hanging, and removing posters in the high school. In the junior high, the executive committees often help the junior high youth worker with the process. CROYA has invested in industrial-size, refillable ink markers, and tries to recycle poster board to keep costs down, but this is an important vehicle for reaching kids as an event nears.

CROYA also posts signs on the community boards in Lake Forest and Lake Bluff. The sign stations are located at busy intersections and serve as an important extra communications tool, especially for parents.

Booklets by CROYA Youth

Every year, CROYA involves young people in producing several booklets that serve as informational pieces for students. The booklets are written and compiled by CROYA youth in conjunction with staff. They're also fun and kid-centered, serving as informal CROYA yearbooks in which active youth can showcase their involvement and get their pictures in, too.

"Everything You Wanted to Know About CROYA but Were Afraid to Ask"

Written and compiled by the senior high executive committee (with a lot of reminding and help from CROYA staff), this booklet does what it claims to do, with youth jargon, humor, and emotion to make it genuine. The process begins in late winter, with the public relations chairs of the executive committee heading up the effort. Each member of the executive committee is asked to write a paragraph that describes his or her position on the committee. It often takes several reminders to get them done, but in the end it's worth it. (See Chapter Four.)

"Who we are. What we are. Why we are."

Similar to the *Everything You Wanted to Know* booklet, this junior high version is prepared at the end of the school year and given out at the annual sixth-grade presentations and other end-of-the-year events. It features a calendar of junior high events through the summer and fall, paragraphs written by kids about meetings and events, and quotes from CROYA youth answering the question "What is CROYA?" Of course, it's also loaded with pictures of kids at all of the past year's CROYA functions. Since newcomers to CROYA don't always understand what it is, this is a great introduction for sixth-graders, presented in a fun, kid-friendly way.

Cable Television

A local cable channel affords the opportunity for regular showings of "CROYA Goes Cable," written and produced by CROYA youth. (See Chapter Seven for details.) Its primary purpose is to inform and educate the public about CROYA, in a hilarious, entertaining manner.

Newsletters

CROYA staff puts updates and upcoming event listings in school and community newsletters and local newspapers. These provide an opportunity to highlight what CROYA is doing, with a paragraph or two promoting new or special events and programs. CROYA also produces its own newsletter several times a year. The impetus is usually an upcoming Adult Board meeting, and the newsletter is used as a pre-meeting vehicle to summarize and highlight for the board members what's been going on and what's coming up. The newsletter is also used as a giveaway at CROYA and at appropriate community meetings.

Publicity and Advertising

Community Meetings

CROYA staffers are often asked to speak at a variety of community meetings, including the American Legion, parent associations, realtor meetings, community-based luncheons, etc. These meetings give CROYA exposure while educating community members about the agency—a win-win for everyone involved.

Publicity

Local newspapers feature articles on CROYA in connection with current events or programs. For example, after Summer Jam or dances, CROYA youth pictures often appear on the cover of the *Lake Forester*, a community newspaper. Staff is proactive in connection with this, calling ahead to staff writers to alert them of upcoming CROYA events.

Advertising

CROYA advertises in local newspapers for events such as the annual poinsettia fundraisers, the rummage sale, and Summer Jam.

Internet

As an agency that is part of the City of Lake Forest, CROYA has its own home page under the city's web address: http://citylf.lfc.edu. CROYA also now has its own website: www.CROYA.com, www.CROYA.net, and www.CROYA.org.

CROYA Brochure

CROYA periodically updates a general brochure about the agency. It describes what CROYA is, the fact that it is youth-driven, its history, and some of the main programs CROYA sponsors.

Good Will and Name Recognition

Meeting Reminder and Thank-You Cards

Used for Adult Board meetings, subcommittee meetings, executive committee meetings, and meetings involving community members, these pre-made postcards are efficient and effective reminders. CROYA also has an artsy thank-you card, designed by a CROYA youth, which is blank inside, and used to send thank-you notes to anyone who participates or helps out in a CROYA function.

Banners

CROYA hangs large plastic banners with the name CROYA (Committee Representing Our Young Adults) in large letters, at all events it sponsors and co-sponsors. This is just another means of advertising and creating and maintaining awareness of CROYA's presence in the community.

14

Organization and Funding

"CROYA's success is not so much dependent on resources as on the willingness of people to recognize that there are problems and come together to solve them."

— Robert Kiely, Lake Forest city manager

Organizational Structure and Financial Resources

CROYA IS FORTUNATE TO BE FUNDED by tax dollars from the City of Lake Forest and the Village of Lake Bluff, as well as schools, regular donations from community organizations, youth-based fundraisers, and occasional private contributions. Its funding base started out modestly, with $10,000 in 1980, and has grown with CROYA as its programming, facilities, and staff have grown over the years. Currently, CROYA's budget comprises 1 percent of the City of Lake Forest's annual operating budget. Of that, approximately 78 percent is allocated for salaries, with the additional monies spent on programming and supplies.

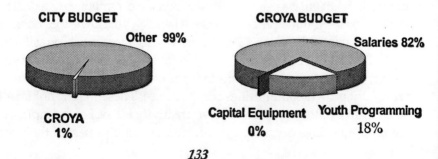

CITY BUDGET

Other 99%

CROYA 1%

CROYA BUDGET

Salaries 82%

Capital Equipment 0%

Youth Programming 18%

133

CROYA's place within the organizational structure of the City of Lake Forest is somewhat unusual in that, despite the fact that CROYA is nongovernmental, it is its own city department. The CROYA director reports directly to the city manager and is a member of the city's executive team, as are the heads of recreation, municipal services, and police and fire, to name a few. This is unusual for this type of agency, with the most logical place seeming to fall under the parks and recreation department, but this arrangement has worked well for CROYA for several reasons. It has alleviated any bureaucracy that might complicate or threaten CROYA's mission. As an independent legal entity, CROYA is responsible for its own budget, accountable for the actions of its staff and youth, and responsible for establishing community connections on its own. This reinforces the significance of the responsibilities with which CROYA representatives are charged. And they live up to that responsibility in their actions, programs, and reputation. Partially as a result of CROYA's success, the Senior Center of Lake Forest is following suit, positioning itself as an independent arm of the city's structure.

Positioning a youth agency under a different city department, such as Parks and Recreation, could also work. In fact, it has been done successfully in other communities, such as Libertyville, Illinois. Their youth agency, called CELYA (Committee Empowering Libertyville's Young Adults) is a part of their Parks and Recreation Department. In operation for nearly five years, they now have a full-time youth worker dedicated to CELYA. She has an office in the Parks and Recreation facility, and the youth group currently has space allocated to it in the town's civic center. (See Chapter Fifteen.)

CROYA's director stresses that what is vital to success is not the organizational and reporting structure but the initial commitment of a staff person and adult community volunteers to the effort. The staff person can be part-time at first, but their sole focus and accountability must be the development of a youth agency that is run by youth. They must be trained and experienced in working with young people, and philosophically committed to the agency's being youth-driven. In addition, it's helpful to look within the community for a dedicated staff person for youth services, someone who knows the town, the people, and most importantly, the youth. (See Chapter Five for more details on staffing.)

While CROYA can be used as a model of how one successful youth agency is structured, it is important for other towns and cities to look within their own communities for resources. These maght not take the same form as CROYA's resources, so creativity is key. For example, other communities have organized youth committees as a part of their social service arms, or as community-based organizations with citizen boards.

In addition to money, the people in every community have a lot to offer in terms of assistance. CROYA has always been successful at tapping into those resources to get the best and most qualified support for its efforts. And community leaders, educators, and residents have been ready and willing to do their part when called upon.

Fundraisers

The CROYA budget covers facilities, staff salaries, programming, and general expenses. For extra things that kids want, such as compact discs, electronics equipment, or extra furnishings, CROYA youth raise money every year through fundraisers. One year they purchased a disco ball, which has been a big hit at CROYA ever since. They also raise money to reupholster the furniture and maintain CROYA's facility, making up for regular wear and tear.

While the staff is involved in each fundraising effort, CROYA youth committee members run the fundraising campaigns via committees. These young leaders are responsible for organization, meetings, and actual fundraising work, such as soliciting community members to support CROYA. These fundraisers, like all CROYA programs, change according to youth interest and involvement. Examples of CROYA's most successful fundraising events follow.

Poinsettia Sale

CROYA's biggest annual fundraiser is the holiday poinsettia sale in November; youth raise as much as $10,000 at this event. Staff meets with a local nursery to choose the plants, then create a brochure and sales packet. Managed primarily by the secretary and staff, young people are encouraged at meetings to sell poinsettias during the pre-holiday season. Cash prizes provide further motivation to be a top money earner.

The CROYA facility is something to see during the week of delivery: Lining the foyer and perimeter of the large room are tables covered with hundreds of poinsettias sorted by size, color, and pickup or delivery date, so careful management is critical. This is where the CROYA secretary comes in, tracking sales and delivery dates, and coordinating pickups and deliveries with staff and students. Parents and community members are big supporters in this consistently successful moneymaker for CROYA.

Rummage Sale

With its first rummage sale last year, CROYA youth raised over $800. The youth committee had voted, prior to the sale, to donate a portion of the money earned to the annual Twin Cities Wisconsin/Chicago AIDS ride, in which several CROYA youth and one staff member were participating. This event took a lot of planning. The subcommittee met often, nagged CROYA kids to clean out their attics, collected rummage, set up, worked the two-day sale, and cleaned up afterward.

Bake Sales and Pizza Sales

Periodically during the school year, CROYA hosts after-school pizza or bake sales. As always, youth help plan the sale, making signs, baking food and working the sale. Baked goods are packaged in sandwich bags in single-size portions, and all are sold for the same price (about 50¢). Pizza, which is ordered from a local pizzeria, is sold for $1.00 a slice. Local pizzerias give discounts on pies to support CROYA, which is why these are good money earners.

Boo Grams

Prior to Halloween, CROYA sells "Boo Grams" at meetings and in the school cafeterias. Here's how it works: Using "Blow Pop" lollypops, wrap the top in a tissue, secure with a rubber band, and draw a face on the head. Students purchase each Boo Gram for 50¢, give the name of the recipient and write a note on a card to be attached. CROYA staff compiles a list and on Halloween (or close to it), sets up in the cafeteria to hand out Boo Grams to students on the list. It's fun for kids, and CROYA makes between $200 and $300 on this fundraiser every Halloween.

Car Washes

Occasionally, CROYA staff and youth will hold a typical fundraising car wash. While washes are free, CROYA accepts donations, and people are usually more than generous. This event comes with pre-wash publicity (signs and maybe ads), lots of elbow grease, and loud music. Kids are fond of this fundraiser, because it gives them a chance to be outside, get wet and be rowdy, but this event comes and goes depending on current youth interest.

✎ Youth Comment on Participating in Fundraisers

"I do it to support CROYA."

"It made me realize that we have to help fund our efforts as well."

"You earn a tee shirt."

"We decide how to use the money."

"It's hard work, but well worth the effort."

"It's a chance to give back."

15

The Future of CROYA
and Our Nation's Youth

⋘⋙

"We have come to the understanding that it is really the process of working with kids that is important—creating a sense of community and goodwill, building positive relationships, supporting each person as an individual human being, building good character, and helping them be the best they can be."

— Kamy Daddono, CROYA director since 1986

Establishing Youth Agencies in Other Communities

CELYA
(Committee Empowering Libertyville's Young Adults)

THE BEST WAY TO MAKE CROYA and other youth organizations live is to help foster new agencies in other communities across the country. This has been done in some neighboring communities, such as Libertyville, Illinois, which is home to CELYA. The Committee Empowering Libertyville's Young Adults has been fortunate in that CROYA's director has worked closely with them for five years to help develop and nurture their youth agency. Starting with a youth commission, which included about seven young people who interviewed for the opportunity, Libertyville spent a year meeting, surveying youth, and talking about ways in which to incorporate a youth program into the community. The commission eventually turned into a mini-youth group after about a year, and demonstrated its viability by putting together a few successful events, such as a coffee house and band jam. The key to CELYA's birth was that community leaders in Libertyville were open-minded, prepared to make the necessary financial commitment, and willing to take some risks.

While Libertyville mirrors in many ways what CROYA does, they have done some things differently in order to align CELYA with their community's goals and organizational structure. For instance, CELYA is housed under the Libertyville Parks and Recreation Department, where CELYA's director has an office. While this was not the route CROYA chose, it's working for CELYA, primarily because they have made the commitment to a dedicated director who is responsible for the youth agency that acts independently from other youth activity programs.

In addition, while CELYA doesn't have its own facility, as CROYA does, they have their own large room located in the civic center, where they get "first dibs" on the space. It is carpeted, with comfortable chairs and pillows strewn about, and is big enough for large meetings or even parties. One of CELYA's first youth-centered projects was to design and paint a mural along the hallway that leads to the CELYA space. Kids are proud of their mural, having made their mark and transformed the civic center, in part, into a kid-friendly place.

A CELYA meeting is reminiscent of a CROYA meeting, with a similar process and rituals, such as initiations, but they've also individualized their program by using meeting agendas and rotating chairpersons semi-annually.

When asked what makes them come back to CELYA, youth reply:

"Friends."
"CELYA helps you get involved with the community."
"It's a place where I'm always welcome. That's a comforting thought."

These could be CROYA youth speaking; they have expressed the very same sentiments again and again. It speaks to common priorities among all young people, and dispels skeptical sentiments about "what is wrong with our nation's youth." Hope lives in the actions and words of young people involved in successful youth communities.

New Generations

CROYA's director has also worked with the town of Barrington, Illinois, to develop their youth initiative, "New Generations," officially begun in 1998. While structured differently than CROYA, they have identified *their* teen needs and priorities, tapping their own community's resources in a manner appropriate for them. High school youth in Barrington meet weekly, as does CROYA, but they are funded differently. While community groups often help financially, youth frequently raise money for individual programs and events of their choosing.

These are examples of how other communities can use the CROYA model, adapting it to their specific demographic and socioeconomic needs and resources. CROYA's philosophies and programs are transferable to other communities across the nation. The real future of CROYA lies in the ability to share and help other villages, towns, municipalities, and cities create their own youth organizations. Other successful models for youth programming have also been documented. *Urban Sanctuaries: Neighborhood Organizations in the Lives and Futures of Inner City Youth,* for example, shares urban models based on similar principals for working with young people, and is an excellent resource.

Evaluating the Success of Youth Programming

"CROYA is asset building—it is prevention at its finest. We are encouraging positive, fun behavior and positive communication skills. CROYA provides a supportive environment and loads of acceptance for everyone!"

— Kris Anderson, parent

As with any organization, agency, or business, effectiveness must be evaluated. Concerned residents want to know that youth programming initiatives are making a difference in their community and the lives of their children. Continued funding hinges on convincing city leaders and taxpayers that the efforts underway are worthwhile.

Representatives from CROYA do not claim to reach all youth in the community, nor do they profess that there are no longer problems with young people. They know that this is not a realistic expectation. Teens still experiment with drugs and alcohol, and struggle with depression, eating disorders, and sexual identity. CROYA feels confident, however, that it reaches a large number of youth, helps circumvent serious teen problems, and provides an invaluable community service.

Independent Research Validates CROYA's Work

As more and more research is compiled and evaluation of existing youth programs is published, it becomes clear that CROYA is on track with youth and has advanced to a higher level of service delivery. In a recent article in *Management Strategy* entitled "Youth Recreation Services: Embracing a New Paradigm for the New Millennium," authors Peter A Witt and John L. Crompton discuss the evolution of youth programming over the past decade.

It seems clear that CROYA is already well advanced in its efforts to meet teen needs. The authors state, for example, "There is now an emphasis on building individual protective factors, resiliency, and community assets and strengths. These models emphasize building the capacity of communities to support the healthy development of youth and treat youth as assets rather than liabilities." CROYA is already doing this. Furthermore, it has embraced, among others, Search Institute's "The Asset Approach," which created the "40 Developmental Assets" as "building blocks of healthy development that help young people grow up healthy, caring, and responsible."[†] CROYA long ago moved beyond targeting "at-risk" youth. Witt and Crompton state, "These models are shifting attention from a problem orientation to [one] based on developing protective factors, assets and resiliency."

They go on to say that, "In many communities, teens have become more adamant about the need for 'places of their own.' The emergence of teen centers run for and by youth is testament to the recognition that process and involvement are important outcomes. Empowering teens helps overcome feelings of helplessness, alienation, and disconnectedness from society and its expectations and standards." CROYA youth have had their facility for thirteen years. More importantly, as has been emphasized throughout this book, CROYA is youth-driven, empowering youth via the CROYA Process.

Further, the fact that CROYA youth workers are well paid and receive good benefits has played a large role in CROYA's success, contributing to worker longevity and continuity of service. As Witt and Crompton point out, "Youth are adversely impacted by unstable funding because it engenders their distrust of involvement with mentors and programs...Inadequate remuneration of youth workers leads to high turnover, and a disruption of mentoring relationships." These mentoring relationships, as CROYA has been fortunate to discover, are essential to establishing trust and caring from which to build self-esteem, self-worth and a sense of fulfillment for young people.

[†] See References, Page 160

Quantitative Evidence

Hard evidence from its own community also suggests that CROYA has successfully addressed some of the initial motivations for its birth—teen suicides and teen gangs. Since the late 1970s, when the community experienced several teen suicides, and was home to a teen gang named The Losers, the community has not experienced a reoccurrence of those problems.

In addition, CROYA has developed its own "Performance Measurement Tracking System" to document and monitor its efforts and effectiveness with youth. This system includes goals, such as the development of new youth programs (many of which are aimed toward at-risk youth), specific performance measures, and tracking columns for measuring quantifiable results. They keep track of how many young people attend different programs and events, and solicit youth feedback regularly. They phase out stale or unpopular programs, improve existing programs, and create new ones yearly, based on youth input. And they are constantly "taking the pulse" of parents, city leaders, and other community members to gauge effectiveness.

Qualitative Evidence

"I am proud to be able to support CROYA's efforts. CROYA not only empowers local youth to create their own programs, service opportunities and social events, they are now reaching out to other communities to share their experience and expertise. This book has the potential to benefit many youth and communities in the State of Illinois."

— Susan Garrett, State Representative
Illinois House of Representatives, 59th District

Perhaps even more compelling is the qualitative evidence of CROYA's success. Attending the annual Recognition Dinner, for instance, one is struck by the obvious impact CROYA has had on the lives of youth involved. (See Chapter Seven.) In the presence of CROYA board members and community leaders, youth speak from the heart about how much CROYA has helped them—from making friends to building self-esteem, from developing leadership qualities to having caring adults to whom to turn. Seniors write moving essays expressing CROYA's impact on their lives and its place in their hearts. (See Chapter Seven and Appendix.) Any doubts about CROYA's effectiveness are dispelled on this memorable evening.

There is even more outside evidence of CROYA's success. CROYA alumni come back to the agency when in town. They keep in touch via e-mail and phone, attend Band Jams or Jell-O Wrestling during holiday breaks, stop by the office to get hugs and catch up with staff, and speak to the impact CROYA has had on their lives as they attend college and move into careers. Parents of current and past "CROYA kids" rave about the positive influence CROYA has had on their children. They urge younger siblings to follow suit by becoming active in the organization.

People also show their appreciation and support in their actions. Community members, local organizations, and state and local government provide additional funds for special projects and programs.(See Acknowledgements.) Carolyn Spadafora gave her time to edit the manuscript because her husband David, president of Lake Forest College, has been on the CROYA board and embraced its work. Countless others made time to interview and come to meetings to offer their memories and insights for this book. Community organizations continue to call yearly for CROYA's youth to participate in community service. Concerned groups throughout the community, such as FOCUS and the Volunteer Bureau, rely on CROYA for input and participation in matters concerning young people. Youth are regularly invited to community-wide meetings and respected for their contributions.

In addition, CROYA's large presence in the schools is always expanding to meet the needs of youth and schools. Faculty and administration develop close working relationships with CROYA staff, attesting to the value of CROYA's important work in the schools. Communities near and far call upon CROYA for advice and assistance in starting their own youth agencies. The CROYA director is frequently asked to speak at forums, seminars, and local meetings. Staff stays on at CROYA, because they love the work and because they know that continuity is important to youth. And taxpayers continue to fund CROYA's effort—one of the strongest indications of CROYA's effectiveness.

As the movement toward more youth communities such as CROYA grows, leaders will continue to develop ways to evaluate effectiveness, as will CROYA and the community it serves. Clearly, the important elements for success are: make the philosophical and financial commitment to a youth agency, find dedicated people to support and nurture the effort, put youth in the driver's seat, and give the agency the time and space to mature and develop. Their effectiveness will be evident in every corner of the youth world and the communities they serve.

Perhaps the greatest testimonial for CROYA's success is in the impact it has had on the lives of the people involved. Their words best capture the essence of CROYA.

"Speaking as an alumna, I don't know how I would have gotten through high school without CROYA. It is here that I formed life-long friendships and learned to have confidence in myself."

— Jill Powell, CROYA alumni

"CROYA sets you up for life. It gives you the ability to make friends and do things. It is a gift that keeps on giving."

— Lucy, CROYA youth

"CROYA is a mature organization that teaches maturity. I matured well beyond my years."

— Scott Grossman, CROYA alumni,
former executive committee chairman

"I've met the most genuine people at CROYA."

—CROYA youth

"CROYA's been the one constant for me."

— Kristina Lazos, CROYA STS Chair

"You always made me feel like it was okay to stay awhile."

— CROYA youth

"I'm so glad to grab hold of something that is so real and so positive."

— Chris Torrence, CROYA vice chair

"CROYA is a really positive escape from things, like homework. CROYA's given me so much. I'm still being offered stepping stones."

— Ashley Engelhart, CROYA youth

"CROYA doesn't condemn. It promotes self-esteem. It affected the way I approached college."

— Amanda Alpert, CROYA alumni
former executive committee McPheeters chair

Looking Ahead for CROYA

As CROYA celebrates its twentieth year and embarks upon a new millennium, it is reevaluating its direction in the face of increased teen violence throughout our nation and cries from community members for more after-school services. Not content to rest on its success, CROYA leaders look to expand services and programming beyond current capacities. As always, however, they are careful to consider any changes, to protect what is at the heart of CROYA and not jeopardize what has become a successful formula for working with youth. They are also cognizant of the need to address the extra burden that expansion would place on staff and facilities.

At a community meeting held to solicit input for this book, parents, school officials, community leaders, and CROYA Adult Board members expressed their desires for the future:

"Be a model to other communities. Being a model will empower it even more."

"Continue with food. CROYA is food!"

"Continue to let kids drive it."

"The evolution should continue."

"Expand staff and add drop-in status with indoor recreational activities available—evening and weekend hours. Activity nights."

At the same time, CROYA hopes, with the publication of this book, to inspire other communities to create youth-centered programming and activities. CROYA plans to develop a web page, perhaps establishing it as an active vehicle for the exchange of ideas among communities moving toward their own "CROYA's." Beyond this, the agency will continue to work with other communities to develop and strengthen youth committees in the early phases, while continuing to deepen its roots in its own community. Most importantly, CROYA will keep doing what it does best, serving the needs of youth, knowing and believing that the seeds it plants will grow beyond its own walls and geographic territory.

Appendix

☙❧

Community Service / Scholarship Letter Sample

[On CROYA Letterhead]
[Date]
[Student's name and address]

Dear   :

We were very happy that you attended the CROYA Spring Retreat under the scholarship program. This program is set up to ensure that any student interested in participating in retreats need not allow financial constraints to get in the way of these fun, educational experiences.

In return for the generous contributions we receive from Lake Forest and Lake Bluff communities that enable us to offer these scholarships, we are asking you to help with the following community service project [Example]:

Lake County Races—April 25, 8:30 A.M. at Lake Bluff train station:

Work at water stations, pass out treat bags to finished runners, direct runners.

Please let me know as soon as possible if you will be able to help. I can be reached at 615-4307.

Sincerely,

[CROYA staff member's name]

Eighth-Grade Tour Questions

1. Was it hard going from junior high to high school?
2. Is there more homework? How much more?
3. Do you have to study harder?
4. How is high school different from junior high? How is it the same?
5. Which do you like better—high school or junior high?
6. Are midterms hard?
7. Is homework required? How much time should you spend on homework to get good grades?
8. Are classes fun or dull?
9. What classes are offered at LFHS?
10. What are honors classes like? A lot more homework? Harder than college prep classes?
11. Is it easy to make new friends?
12. Are there a lot of dances and extra activities at high school?
13. Do you meet a lot of new people?
14. Do you still go on school trips?
15. What do you do at CROYA as high school students?
16. Is it hard to find your way around the school? Do they give you maps?
17. Will upper-classmen help freshmen, or pick on them?
18. How do you get to class on time without any bells? How much time in between classes?
19. What's the hardest thing about the first day?
20. Can we eat and drink food in class? Can I listen to my Walkman?
21. Do you recommend getting involved in sports and clubs? Which ones? Is it hard to get on sports teams or join the clubs?
22. Are drugs or guns a problem at high school?
23. Do senior guys really pick on the freshman girls?
24. How many students are there?
25. Are there lots of cliques at high school? Are we going to get labeled as "preppies", etc.
26. If high school is so much fun, why does it sound like so much work?
27. Are the school lunches disgusting? Can you eat off campus?
28. How long does it take you to finally know your way around the whole school?

29. How long are the class periods?

30. Are the teachers really strict about following the rules? Will the teachers help you?

31. What's the biggest thing you have to prepare for?

32. Is there any free time at all, or is it all homework and studying?

33. How do you get involved with Student Council?

34. Does the high school have summer school courses?

35. How would you sum up high school?

36. What time does school start? Can you drive to school once you're a junior?

37. Can you be in the school play as a freshman? Is there a drama club?

38. Should you go to your locker after every class or carry a backpack?

39. Do you keep your friends from Jr. High or do you change friends?

40. What are finals like? How often do you have to do term papers?

41. Is it hard to do sports and keep your grades up?

42. Do people get detentions or do they do something different in high school?

Excellent Adventure Flyer and Permission Slip Samples
Seventh- And Eighth-graders
Croya's Most Excellent Adventure

DATE: Saturday, April 10, 10:00 A.M.–7:00 P.M. (with option to stay for a movie or open gym until 9:00 P.M.
PLACE: CROYA, 400 Hastings Rd. We will be going to the Northbrook Teams Challenge Course from noon to 4:00 P.M., traveling by bus.
PRICE: $35.00 for the whole day—lunch, dinner, challenge course, transportation, surprises included!
    **Scholarships available
BRING: Warm, comfortable clothing, a change of clothes, a snack to share with everyone (enough for 25 people). April weather is very unpredictable, so watch the news and be prepared!

For more information, call CROYA at 615-4304.

**SPACE IS LIMITED TO 60 STUDENTS AND IS GIVEN ON A FIRST-COME, FIRST-SERVED BASIS!
THIS PERMISSION SLIP MUST BE RETURNED BY APRIL 6TH.

Permission Slip
_____has my permission to go on the CROYA's Most Excellent Adventure on April 10. I understand that my child will be transported by bus to the Northbrook Park District and that those in charge will use every precaution for the safety of the students. However, in the case of an accident or emergency, I will not attempt to hold CROYA, the City of Lake Forest or the Village of Lake Bluff in any way responsible. **I have read and agree with the Liability Waiver on the back.**

_____

Signature of Parent/Guardian   Date

_____

Attending Junior High   Telephone

Excellent Adventure Friendship Worksheet

Directions: Fill this star with words describing the qualities you look for in a friend.

Think of two or three people you consider friends.
Do they exhibit those characteristics?
Which of those qualities do you have?

_____

Which of those qualities do you need to improve on in order to acquire more friends? _____
Name one person in this group you would like to get to know better.

_____

Tell how you intend to go about this.

_____

Excellent Adventure Questions for Small Group Discussion

[Note: cut up and put strips into bag for each group]

What do you do when you're fighting with your parents and you feel they're being unfair to you?

What is the hardest thing in your life right now? How are you dealing with it?

Do you have any friends that you always worry about?

How is your relationship with your family?

What do you like to do to lift your spirits?

What is the wildest or most outrageous thing you have done or would like to do?

What is the greatest challenge in your life?

What talent would you most like to have?

If you were in the Olympics, which event would you most like to compete in?

If you could be either the most attractive, the most athletic, or the smartest kid in your class, which would you choose and why?

What is most important now?

If you had only five minutes to think up a nickname for yourself and knew everyone would use it for years, what would you pick?

What habits would you like to eliminate in yourself? In others?

What do you like about your appearance?

If you could grow up to be famous and successful, what would you like to be known for?

What is the hardest thing about growing up?

If your home was on fire and you had time to grab only two things, what would they be?

What are some accomplishments, small or large, that you are proud of?

What do you see yourself doing in three years? Five years?

When I grow up I am going to be...

The greatest treasure in my life is...

Who are your heroes and mentors?

What do you always find time for? What do you never seem to find time for?

If you could have any job in the world, what would it be?

If you had only thirty-five cents, whom would you call?

Where in the world would you move to tomorrow? Why?

What was some of the most interesting or useful information you learned today?

What are some of the reasons why physical appearance is so important to teens?

How can a person better accept his/her changing appearance during adolescence?

What can I do if I like a person or group and they don't like me?

What can I do for a friend who has problems?

What should I do if good friends of mine are doing things that I believe are wrong?

If a friend is in serious trouble (e.g., drugs, bulimia) and confides in me, what do I do?

What causes teenagers to get depressed? How can you prevent it?

What can a person do when he/she gets depressed?

What are your feelings about the coming years of your life and the choices you will be making?

What is a concern for you in your life today?

Have you ever stood up for something and gone against your friends? What happened?

Do you have any fears in life?

Is there something you really look forward to?

If you could change one thing about yourself, what would it be? Why?

If you could do something over again, what would it be?

Excellent Adventure Tree Collage Activity

Through this activity, you will be thinking and reflecting on your life. Try to come up with thoughts and feelings for each symbol. If you do not want to share certain feelings, that's OK.

Symbols for Tree
  Bee—Fears
  Leaves—Dreams
  Flower—Memories
  Sun—What makes you happy
  Tree trunk—Hobbies

NOTE: CROYA staff provides paper cutouts (3–4" diameter) in the shape of bees, leaves, and flowers that will eventually be affixed to the tree trunk. The large tree trunk (about six feet high) is made with brown paper and divided into as many pieces as there will be small groups. The same is done for the sun, which is divided into pie-shaped sections. Each person gets a bee, a leaf and a flower on which to inscribe her thoughts and feelings. Each group gets a piece of the trunk and the sun, which are later joined with the other groups' sections. Then, the leaves, bees and flowers are connected to the tree trunk on a wall, so that everyone's ideas and learning come together to form a beautiful tree.

Retreat Permission and Medical Form

_____ has my permission to go on the CROYA Fall Retreat being held Friday, November 5 through Sun., November 7, at B'nai B'rith Beber Camp, Mukwonago, Wisconsin. I understand that my child will be transported by bus to the retreat center and that those in charge will use every precaution for the safety of the students. However, in the case of an accident or emergency, I will not attempt to hold CROYA, the City of Lake Forest or Village of Lake Bluff in any way responsible. **I have read and agree with the Liability Waiver on the back.**

Parent/Guardian _____

Phone_____

Date _____

As the Parent/Guardian of _____, I give my explicit permission for any of the adult staff on the CROYA Encounters Retreat to authorize any emergency medical procedure and to obtain medical prescriptions as necessary to treat any medical problem, sickness, or accident incurred during the weekend of November 5–7.

Date_____

Signature of Parent/Guardian_____

Insurance Company & Policy

#_____

*Please indicate any allergies: _____

*Please list any medication the student is required to take during the Retreat:_____

*Complete name, address and phone number of Parent/Legal Guardian who can be called in case of an emergency during the Retreat:

Name _____

Address_____

Phone_____

*Name of someone who may be contacted in case the Parent / Guardian cannot be reached:

Name_____

Address_____

Phone_____

_____Here is my non-refundable deposit of $25.00, with the remaining $55.00 to be paid on or before [deadline date], at the CROYA facility before leaving.

_____Here is the total fee of $ 80.00 ($ 25.00 being a non-refundable deposit)

_____Here is my non-refundable fee of $50.00 for two students in one family, with the remaining ($ 110.00 to be paid on or before [deadline date] at the CROYA facility before leaving).

Participant Liability Waiver And Hold Harmless Agreement

Please read this form carefully and be aware that by registering for and participating in this program or by registering your minor child/ward for participation in this program, you will be waiving your rights and/or the rights of your minor child/ward to all claims for injuries that you or your minor child/ward might sustain arising out of this program, and you will be required to indemnify, hold harmless and defend CROYA, the City of Lake Forest, and the Village of Lake Bluff for any claims arising out of participation in said program.

Risk in Injury: As a participant in the program, or as a parent or legal guardian of a participant under eighteen years of age, I recognize and acknowledge that there are certain risks of physical injury. I agree to assume the full risk of injuries, including death, damages, or loss that I may sustain as a result of participating in any and all activities associated with this program.

Waiver of Injury Claims: I agree to waive and relinquish any and all claims I may have arising out of, connected with, or in any way associated with the activities of the program.

Release from Liability: I do hereby fully release and discharge CROYA, the City of Lake Forest and Village of Lake Bluff and its officers, agents, and employees from any and all claims from injuries, including death, damage, or loss, that I or my minor child/ward may have or that may occur on account of participation in the program.

Indemnity and Defense: I further agree to indemnify, hold harmless and defend CROYA, City of Lake Forest and Village of Lake Bluff and its officers, agents, and employees from any and all claims from injuries, including death, damages, and losses sustained by me or my minor child/ward and arising out of, connected with, or in any way associated with the activities of the program.

In the event of any emergency, I authorize CROYA to secure from any licensed hospital, physician, and/or medical personnel any treatment deemed reasonable and necessary for my minor child's immediate care and agree that I will be responsible for payment of any and all medical services rendered.

I have read and fully understand and agree to the above Participant Liability Waiver and Hold Harmless Agreement.

Parent or Guardian
Signature _____

Date _____

Retreat "What to Bring" List (Weekend Retreats)

1. Towel
2. Pillow
3. Sleeping bag or twin sheets and a blanket
4. Warm and comfortable clothes
5. Gym clothes and shoes
6. Bring enough liquid to keep you hydrated (i.e., water, juice, soda)
7. A treat to share with everyone (enough for thirty people). Please make half of it healthy (apples, granola, muffins, etc.)
8. Toiletry supplies for good grooming, including soap, toothbrush and toothpaste
9. Warm jacket, gloves and shoes
10. Camera
11. Any games or a deck of cards for spare time
12. Flashlight
13. A movie (we have access to a VCR)
14. A candle that stands alone or has a holder!
15. Magazines
16. An object that has a special meaning to you!

**PLEASE be very conservative on supplies. Bring *one* bag if possible. We have very limited space on the bus.

Senior Essay Scholarship Contest

$1,000 scholarship Essay Contest
Dear Seniors,

Just wanted to let you know we're accepting entries for the "Spirit of CROYA" Senior Essay Contest this week. If you are interested in entering the contest, please write 1–3 pages expressing what CROYA has meant to you. These essays can take on any form you wish, from personal accounts to stories, to anything creative you come up with. They are due at CROYA by this Wednesday, April 28th at 8:00 P.M. If you want to enter the contest, but feel you need more time, call Todd at CROYA immediately (phone #). Students will read all the essays and vote on which are the best.

1 essay will win a $1,000 scholarship

OR

2 essays will win a $500 scholarship

The award(s) will be given out at the Recognition Dinner on May 10th at Gorton Community Center.

Good Luck, The CROYA Staff

Senior Essay Voting Procedures
Dear CROYA Senior Essay Readers:

Please read through all of the essays. Then pick three that stand out as the best representation of what "The Spirit of CROYA" means to you.

If you figure out who has written the essays, please do not let that influence which ones you feel are the best.

Rank the three best: 1st, 2nd, 3rd.

Call Todd's voice mail (phone #) and vote for 1st, 2nd and 3rd.

Please call to vote by Sunday night. If you have any ?'s, leave me a message and I will call you back.

Thanks for all your help.
Todd

Senior Essay Sample
CROYA Scholarship Winning Essay

By Jane Nelson

> *"I expect to pass through this place but once. Any good therefore that I can do, or any kindness that I can show to any fellow creature, let me do it now, for I shall not pass this way again."*

— Author unknown

There is something remarkable about giving—it seems the more you do it, the more you gain. Oddly enough, in today's society, particularly that of my peers, it seems as if we have been groomed not to give too much, not to let others know you care, not to get too close to anyone. "Don't depend on any person, and you'll never get hurt," seems to be the safeguard today. These thoughts are what lead to the eventual breakdown of so many of my peers today—and these are all problems tackled daily by a unique organization called CROYA.

"How does CROYA do this?" I've been asked this very question numerous times. The answer is really quite simple—CROYA is the only program designed specifically for the enjoyment and benefit of its members – the youth. In attempting to establish programs for the body of CROYA, this network has managed to create a warm, safe environment where all members are valued. The youth come to CROYA because they are respected at CROYA. In turn, its members want to give, want to work, and want to succeed at any endeavors they take on.

In addition to its workability, CROYA's atmosphere promotes yet another much-needed facet with today's kids—friendships. I've experienced it first-hand—the jock becomes friends with the nerd, the freshman with the upperclassman—and I am convinced that this strength can only be attributed to the remarkable leadership found in our organization.

The staff at CROYA is dedicated to the pursuit of *our* happiness and *our* pride in our programs. The time and devotion each employee—Mrs. M., Kamy, and Dan—brings to our activities is what makes them succeed. Without these incredible role models, friends, and confidantes to assist us, CROYA would not have become the incredible organization it is today.

Each member finds something different in CROYA. This multifaceted characteristic of our programs is one of the greatest strengths we have. Personally, I have attempted to participate in nearly all of CROYA's different areas, and in my four years at CROYA, have grown to hold considerable esteem for the amazing things we have going on. Physically, mentally, and spiritually, I have grown up quite a bit during my high school career. However, the greatest factor in my personal growth must be attributed to my experiences within CROYA.

I entered my freshman year insecure and self-conscious, afraid to speak in front of even five or six people. Unsure of why I was going through the near-fatal INITIATION at CROYA, I did it anyway. But as the school year took off, so did my involvement with CROYA. After attending the first-ever Fall Retreat, I was convinced that somehow I had almost accidentally walked into the program for me. Inside the walls of CROYA, I was valued, respected, and liked—even by those upperclassmen!

The Close Encounters program taught me things about other people, and skills that I will use for the rest of my life. As my dedication to the field experiences increased, I began to trust my own ability as a friend, listener, and leader, and felt equally touched by each individual I came in contact with. As Close Encounters chairman, I gained a deeper understanding of the amazing potential we had within this program. Gone were the stereotypical Lake Forest teens, replaced by some of the most inspirational, devoted, and caring youth I will ever have the opportunity to work with.

This year, as chairman of CROYA, I have acquired so many treasures—be it a better understanding of others, the skills of motivating and representing a large organization, or just an incredibly increased sense of self-confidence. Serving on the CROYA board and working with the members of our city's government and various other adults has made me realize what a wonderful gift our community has given us.

We have a truly amazing program at our fingertips—I know that, as do most who have ever participated in any of our programs. And no matter what amount of involvement any given member dedicates to CROYA, my hope is that they have all been touched by the spirit of CROYA. As much as I am ready to leave LFHS and experience college life, leaving the organization that I know so well, and the incredible relationships I have established here, is going to be one of the hardest things I have ever had to do. I don't believe that I will ever find another group with so many people I love, anywhere. The magic of CROYA has touched me—deeply—in a place very few have ever reached. The one hope I leave behind is for the future of CROYA: Realize how and why we've become what we are today and keep that magic alive. Through the years, members and staff may enter and leave the doors of CROYA, but so long as their memories are alive in the hearts of its leaders, CROYA will never die.

Senior High Youth Group Executive Committee Requirements
General Requirements

Must: 1. Actively attend a majority of CROYA functions.

2. Be able to stay in touch with the senior high youth worker (staff) and the chair of the executive committee.

3. Represent CROYA with a smile!

Executive Committee: *Chairperson*

Must: 1. Be a senior.

2. Have previously held a position on the executive committee.

3. Be actively involved with STS/CROYA Encounters and the Youth Committee.

Vice Chair

Must: 1. Be a junior or a senior.

2. Have chaired a subcommittee.

Fundraiser Chairs (2)

Must: 1. Be a sophomore, junior, or senior.

2. Have chaired a subcommittee.

Topic Night Chairs (2)

Must: 1. Be a sophomore, junior or senior.

2. Position open to entire Youth Committee.

Public Relations Chairs (2)

Must: 1. Be a sophomore, junior, or senior.

2. Position open to entire Youth Committee.

McPheeters Chairs [games and fun things] (2)

Must: 1. Be a junior or senior.

2. Have chaired a subcommittee.

Parliamentarians (2)

Must: 1. Elect one girl and one guy who are either juniors or seniors.

2. Position open to entire Youth Committee.

Poster Board Chair (1)

Must: 1. Be a sophomore or junior.

2. Position open to entire Youth Committee.

Cable Chairs (2)

Must: 1. Be a sophomore, junior or senior.

2. Be willing to be trained on cable equipment.

STS/Croya Encounters Committee Chair

Must: 1. Be a senior.

2. Have completed Peer Training.

3. Have attended a CROYA retreat.

4. Be currently involved in field experiences.

Vice Chairs (2)

Must: 1. Be a junior or senior

2. Have completed Peer Training.

3. Be currently involved in field experiences.

References

⊂੪੨⊃

The Asset Approach: Giving Kids What They Need to Succeed. Copyright © 1977 by Search Institute, 700 S. Third Street, Suite 210, Minneapolis, MN 55415. All Rights Reserved.

Hennessy, John, Farwell, Frank II, Fischbach, John. *The Report of the Ad Hoc Committee on Youth Matters to The Lake Forest City Council,* June 1980.

Hotchkiss, Eugene. *The Committee Representing Our Young Adults: An Evaluation and Assessment.* 1986.

McLaughlin, Milbrey W., Irby, Merita A., and Langman, Julie. *Urban Sanctuaries: Neighborhood Organizations in the Lives and Futures of Inner-City Youth.* San Francisco: Jossey-Bass Publishers, 1994.

Muehlbauer, Gene; Eskilson, Arlene; and Dodder, Laura. *Youth Needs Assessment: A Report to the Committee Representing Our Young Adults of Lake Forest and Lake Bluff,* 1981.

Scales, Peter C. *A Portrait of Young Adolescents in the 1990s.* Minneapolis, MN: Search Institute, 1995.

Witt, Peter A. and Crompton, John L. *Youth Recreation Services: Embracing a New Paradigm for the New Millennium.* Sagamore Publishing, Vol. 23, No. 4, Winter 1999.

Additional Reading

Carrell, Susan. *Group Exercises for Adolescents: A Manual for Therapists.* Newbury Park, CA: Sage Publications, Inc., 1993. [ISBN# 0-8039-5292-9]

Eckert, Larry. *If anybody asks me...1001 Questions for educators, counselors and therapists.* Oklahoma City: Wood & Barnes Publishing, 1998. [ISBN# 1-885473-24-9]

Frey, Diane and Carlock, c. Jesse. *Practical Techniques for Enhancing Self-Esteem.* Bristol, PA: Accelerated Development, 1991. [ISBN# 1-55959-009-2]

Khalsa, SiriNam S. *Group Exercises for Enhancing Social Skills & Self Esteem.* Sarasota, FL: Professional Resource Press, 1996. [ISBN# 1-56887-020-5]

Teolis, Beth. *Ready to Use Self-Esteem & Conflict-Solving Activities for Grades 4-8.* West Nyack, NY: The Center for Applied Research in Education, 1996. [ISBN# 0-7628-611-2]

ORDER FORM

To order additional copies of *Empowering Teens*,
photocopy and complete this order form, and send or fax it to:

CROYA   Fax (847) 615-4251
400 Hastings Road   Phone (847) 615-4304
Lake Forest, IL 60045   www.CROYA.com

Shipping Address:

_____

(Name)

_____

(Street Address)

_____

(City)   (State)   (ZIP)

Quantity

Please send me [   ] copies at $19.95 per book .... Sub._____
Shipping and Handling:
$3.00 for one book, $1. per additional copy,
($0.50 per copy if ordering more than 10)
International orders: $10.00, $1.00 per additional copy. .... S/H._____
Illinois residents, please add 6.5% sales tax .... Tax:_____

☐ Enclosed is a check in the amount of .... TOTAL:_____
☐ Please charge my credit card for the above amount.

We accept   ☐ Visa or ☐ Mastercard (please select your card)

Card number_____   Expiration Date _____

Signature _____   Date_____